WINNING SALES LETTERS—
FROM PROSPECT TO CLOSE

Ralph Allora

McGraw Hill

New York   Chicago   San Francisco   Lisbon   London
Madrid   Mexico City   Milan   New Delhi   San Juan
Seoul   Singapore   Sydney   Toronto

1 2 3 4 5 6 7 8 9 0 FGR/FGR 0 1 0 9

ISBN: 978-0-07162811-2
MHID: 0-07-162811-8

McGraw-Hill books are available at special quantity discounts to use as premiums and sales promotions, or for use in corporate training programs. To contact a representative please e-mail us at bulksales@mcgraw-hill.com.

Library of Congress Cataloging-in-Publication Data

Allora, Ralph.
    Winning sales letters from prospect to close / by Ralph Allora.
      p. cm.
    ISBN 978-0-07-162811-2 (alk. Paper)
1. Sales letters. 2. Selling. 3. Electronic mail messages. I. Title.
    HF5730.A56 2010
    658.8'1—dc22

                                                                    2009011084

Contents

CONTENTS

Acknowledgments

Special thanks to Donya Dickerson at McGraw-Hill, who championed the idea for this book and whose skillful editing shaped it into an ideal form; to Angelica Carey, whose keen eye and business savvy I have long relied on to help make me a better communicator; to Christopher Caudwell and Bob Lonigro, two of the best sales professionals I know, who gave me priceless insight into the psychology of successful deal-making; to Amber, whose love sustained me throughout the writing process; to my father, who instilled in me the confidence to pursue my life's ambitions; and to my mother, who has always encouraged me to do my best work.

Introduction

Does your sales job cause you anxiety? You're not alone. According to a 2008 survey by SalesDog.com, an online educational resource for sales professionals, nearly 6 in 10 sales professionals consider their job to be high-stress. When the economy is sour, everyone's desperately fighting for a piece of a rapidly dwindling pie. And when times are flush, management ratchets up the pressure on its sales staff to produce numbers even greater than the previous year's.

Whether you're a salesperson or a small-business owner whose responsibilities include pitching your services directly to customers, your job isn't getting any easier. You're no longer up against just a narrowly defined set of competitors; you're contending with fast-evolving technologies and ever-expanding choices for your target audience on where and how it spends its money.

No matter how localized or specialized your product or service, your competition is broader and more agile than ever before. If you're selling real estate, for example, you're no longer just up against other local agents; you're also dealing with Web-based Realty services. If you're pitching customer-service solutions, you're doing so against lean and nimble companies scattered around the globe.

But you have at least one thing in your corner: the ability to develop and maintain warm, trusting, personalized business relationships with your clients. In the end, that's really all that counts. This book begins with the premise that you, as a striving sales professional or motivated entrepreneur, are good with people—after all, it's why you do what you do for a living.

Let's go a step further and assume that you've gone through the face-to-face drill so many times that you can do it without breaking a sweat: You walk into your client's office bearing a genial grin and a firm handshake, you sit down with him or her, and you proceed to confidently and clearly lay out your company's sales pitch. You have the facts straight, your delivery is polished, and your personality shines through, helping you bond with the person across the desk. Thirty minutes later, that person is mightily impressed and is one big step closer to doing business with you.

In short, you're a proficient oral communicator, and you've been relying on that skill to make the difference with your customers. In a moment of quiet reflection, though, you'd probably admit that your most formidable competitors—the ones whose names vexingly keep coming up in those management meetings—are pretty good on the phone and in meetings too. They're in this business for the same reasons you are.

Therefore, if you could add another dimension to your communication skills—one that your competitors likely haven't spent too much time thinking about and one that could help you to foster all-important trust with your clients—would you not embrace it? More to the point, if you're locked in a fierce battle for a piece of new business, for market share, or for the hearts and minds of customers, wouldn't you want every possible advantage at your disposal?

Well, you just picked up one little advantage: The preceding paragraph contains two examples of the rhetorical question—a powerful psychological tool that helps to move a person to your point of view. It's a prime case for what can be accomplished with an often-overlooked aspect of sales communication: the well-crafted sales letter or e-mail. And it's one of the many writing devices and techniques you'll pick up from this book.

THE SKILL THAT SETS YOU APART

If you've never put much time or thought into letters and e-mails to potential customers, well, your competitors probably haven't either. In sales, writing is an undervalued skill. My background happens to be in the world of publishing and media, and even there—a field in which written content and information are key components of the *products* being sold—I encountered many salespeople who would rather have given up their travel and entertainment (T&E) allowances than write an actual letter to a client.

But anyone who leaves this skill undeveloped is missing the power of the well-written sales message. When you're entering that tentative discovery phase with a prospective customer, a series of thoughtful sales notes can go a long way toward cementing the relationship. These notes are also an invaluable opportunity to show the prospect how you think and how you approach his or her business.

As you know, your clients don't have a whole lot of time for you. This is why you should consider the sales note to be a prime tool in your kit, just as important as an across-the-desk meeting. It's your calling card and a crucial way to stay on customers' radar.

By writing an effective introductory letter, you're creating a more efficient selling scenario. In other words, the letter or e-mail can do a lot of the hard work for you. When you finally sit down in front of that prospect, you've already laid the groundwork for the meeting, so your relationship starts off at a higher functioning level. You're in a position to start reinforcing—not introducing—your key sales points.

Throughout the negotiation process and into closing the deal, the persuasively written note can add substance and authority to your claims. Once the contract is signed and you're in client-service mode, a brief, meaningful note in your client's inbox makes a statement that you're still working hard to keep his or her business.

Having said all this, I'll be the first to admit that written communication is not the magic bullet for closing a sale. A letter or e-mail, no matter how well developed, is simply no substitute for face-to-face contact. It's not unlike online dating. You can exchange witty, flirtatious e-mails with another person forever, but until you make plans to actually meet at the local café, you're technically still alone. Use the sales letter to open the door and make yourself known—and continue using it to communicate important information—but as soon as you can, get on the phone and make an appointment. As you move through the various stages of the sale, consider these written messages to be a *supplement* to your face-to-face conversations, not a replacement for them.

LETTERS VERSUS E-MAIL

Something else to think about: While most likely you'll be making your sales points through a series of smart, finely tuned e-mails, don't underestimate the impact of kicking off the customer relationship by sending a real, printed-on-pulp letter.

In the hyperspeed environment of modern business—and in an eco-conscious age that discourages the excessive use of paper—you might ask whether sending an old-fashioned printed letter is even relevant or necessary. The answer is yes, at least in certain cases. When a prospect receives a posted letter that appears to be legitimate business correspondence and not junk mail, he or she usually will feel compelled to at least open and skim through it. It's an act that requires more conscious effort than a mouse click.

Another factor is the issue of intrusiveness. When an e-mail appears in someone's inbox, it's usually accompanied by a *ding* or a pop-up notice while the person is in the middle of working. You run the risk of the prospect being irritated by the interruption. A printed letter, on the other hand, doesn't drop from the ceiling onto the recipient's head; it's opened when he or she is ready to check the mail.

The tradeoff, of course, is that you usually can't tell whether a printed letter has been received and read; with an e-mail, you can (if you set up a receipt notification). A prospect may feel more compelled to respond to an e-mail because it's spontaneous and immediate, as opposed to a printed letter, which seems a bit more removed.

My advice is to consider a typed, printed note as your introduction and then follow up by phone. Once you've made a personal connection with the prospect, you're free to switch the dialogue to e-mail. Finally, when the deal is complete and it's time for your thank-you note, switch back to paper. (Just try to use the recycled kind.)

WHAT'S SO HARD ABOUT WRITING?

Back to the original premise, then. Given the idea that most ambitious sales professionals and entrepreneurs are naturals at face-to-face and phone interactions with clients, why do so many avoid attempts to make a similar impression in e-mails or on paper?

The antiwriting society tends to fall into two camps. The first group just doesn't want to be bothered with written sales communications. These businesspeople, no matter how successful, consider writing to be a hassle or an inconvenience. They think, sure, I'd love to be able to write a decent sales letter, but it takes too long. An hour spent drafting a letter is an hour taken away from my face time with clients, which is where I make my money. If you're in this camp, you have a legitimate concern. However, if you devise a strategy before you hit the keyboard, you'll find that it takes less and less time to write. Do a few letters, and it will soon become as natural a part of your daily routine as your morning cup of coffee.

The second group, prompted by flashbacks to some particularly painful episode in eighth-grade English class, has an irrational fear of writing. These otherwise unflappable pros agonize over the simplest note. If you're one of them, take a deep breath and relax. While some people are born great writers, the other 99.99 percent of us have to work at it. And your job isn't to be Shakespeare or Faulkner. Nor is it to impress your clients with 10-dollar SAT words. Your job, simply, is to *communicate in your own voice*. Basically, if you can speak and read, you can write. If you're comfortable schmoozing in person or over the phone—and you know you are—writing shouldn't be such a nightmare.

WHAT MAKES FOR A GOOD SALES LETTER?

At the risk of sounding obvious, the effective sales note contains a message that gets noticed and acted on. Whether you send it electronically or on paper, your message is a drop in the sea of e-mails and posted mail—much of it junk that gets deleted or tossed instantly—that your prospect receives every day. So you have no choice but to break through the clutter. Just as with your face-to-face or phone conversations, your letters must be articulate and understandable, command attention, motivate your client or customer to take action, and stick in his or her mind.

In the space of six or seven short paragraphs on a sheet of paper or in an e-mail message, you should be able to convey all the emotional punch, persuasiveness, and brand positioning of a 30-minute face-to-face sales call or client meeting.

This book is designed to help guide the way, with tips on how to get over any aversion to writing you might have and how to craft great, high-impact sales letters and e-mails that can give you a clear edge over the competition.

Within these pages, you'll learn the essentials of sound letter structure, from the core idea to the call to action. You'll pick up the rules for bringing a message to life, as well as timely secrets to effective e-mails and text messages from mobile devices. At the heart of this book are what I call *deal-makers*—insider techniques that get clients not just to read a letter but also to take action on it. You'll get situational strategies for messages throughout every stage of the selling process from the introductory note, through price negotiation, to follow-up client service. You'll even find a grammar and usage crib sheet to avoid pesky mistakes and keep your letters smart and professional.

Finally, you've probably heard the old saying about the difference between giving a man a fish to eat and teaching him how to fish. This book will endeavor to accomplish both. In addition to the advice that will help you go out and cast for customers, you'll get plenty of "fish" for your consumption—a wide variety of sample letters that bring the concepts home.

It's time to sharpen the skill that can put you top-of-mind among your customers. If you're ready to commit your message to paper—or an e-mail server—remember that the spoken word is fleeting; the written word is permanent. This book will help to make sure that you get it right.

A FEW NOTES

1. The tips and techniques described in this book can be used by sales professionals looking to boost their business prospects, by small-business owners who don't have the luxury of a sales or marketing staff to present their companies' case, or by anyone else whose goal is to get a specific target audience to take a specific action. They also apply whether your market is trade or con-

sumer, for-profit or nonprofit. (Many points are illustrated by using two examples: one for a business-to-business audience and one for a consumer audience.)

2. Apart from presenting some basic sales principles, this book does not purport to teach the finer nuances of selling. It begins with the assumption that you, the reader, have other sources for acquiring knowledge on the art of prospecting and negotiating, for example. It simply presents advice on how to further one's sales skills through writing at all stages of the process.

3. This book also assumes that you've done your homework prior to making a cold call. In other words, you've confirmed that the prospect is the right decision maker (or at least an appropriate first point of contact on the road to the final decision), you've looked into what your competition is doing in this market, you've done research on the prospect's market or industry, and you know at least the basic facts about the prospect's business, demographics, or buying behavior. If you haven't done this yet, you're probably not ready to begin crafting an effective introductory note.

4. A number of the highlighted techniques in this book come from the world of direct marketing and are aimed squarely at a reader's emotions. But, you might say, my audience is a group of sober-minded, spreadsheet-obsessed suits with no apparent lives outside the office. Why make an emotional pitch? The reason: No matter who your targets are—doctors, purchase managers, information technology (IT) executives, homeowners, or pet lovers—they are all human beings who respond best to personal, gut-level appeals.

5. Throughout this book I use the terms *letter*, *note*, and *message* interchangeably, sometimes when referring to e-mails. This is so because many of the basic rules apply for both e-mails and printed letters. However, e-mail writing is its own artform, with considerations for length (e-mails need to be even more concise in their language) and the use of subject lines versus letter headlines, to name a couple. Thus I've devoted a separate chapter to e-mails and text messages from mobile devices.

6. On many pages you'll see a text passage presented within a box. This is to highlight an example of language that might appear in a sales letter or e-mail. Please note, however, that while most of these passages represent examples of effective and/or correct usage of language (the ones you want to follow), some indicate examples of *incorrect* or *poor* usage (the ones you want to avoid in your letters). To make certain which is which, please refer to the lead-in text directly preceding the box—it should be self-explanatory. Within some of the boxed text passages you'll see bold or italicized words or phrases—unless otherwise noted, these are to emphasize a specific rule or point only and should not be replicated in your own sentences.

With that, let's get started.

Chapter 1

The Essentials:
Sound Letter Structure

You wouldn't start a business without first hammering out a plan. You wouldn't call a meeting without first establishing an agenda. So why would you sit down at your desk with your fingers hovering over the keyboard if you haven't put a little thought into the structure of your written sales message?

You're probably anxious to get right to the juicier stuff—the hot-button techniques that help to sway opinion and influence action. Before you can truly sculpt your work of art, though, you need to be able to manipulate the raw materials correctly. This chapter will show you how to chip away at the rough form of your message—the starting point for crafting an effective, professional-looking introductory letter.

ORGANIZATION

Preparing to write a sales letter or an e-mail isn't too dissimilar from thinking about how you'll present your oral pitch in a sales call or customer meeting. Just as various types of sales calls have different objectives, so too does the written note, whether it's an introductory letter, a follow-up on a call, or an e-mail addressing a specific objection. What these messages have in common is that they must address four key questions, all of which you should consider before you start typing:

1. What is the problem or challenge faced by my client or prospect?

This can be answered through the same homework you'd undertake for any client call. As stated in the introduction, it's a given that you'll need to do the research on the customer's needs, analyze the competitive set, and read the trade reports.

Examples of some issues that your prospect might be facing include

- Rising costs
- Inferior service from suppliers
- Shrinking market share
- Information overload
- Lack of time

2. What is it about my product, service, or business proposal that helps to solve the problem?

If you're representing a larger organization, this answer usually is found in training materials, the corporate Web site, press releases, and other resources or through discussions with management or coworkers. (You might have to dig a bit—sometimes, unfortunately, the core message is buried.) If you're completely on your own, use your judgment, and bounce ideas off trusted industry colleagues.

Examples of how you can help to solve the problem include

- Provide great value.
- Provide superior service.
- Provide high quality.
- Provide productivity-enhancing technology.
- Provide versatility of use.

3. What do I want the client or prospect to do as a result of reading this message?

This is the call to action. Based on where you are in the selling process, think carefully about the *specific* action you want the client to take after he or she finishes reading the note.

Examples of a call to action include

- Visit our Web site.
- Read our brochure.
- Make an appointment with us.
- Buy our product/service online.
- Consider our latest offer.
- Try our free demo.

4. What in this message will specifically benefit the client or prospect?

It's one thing to make a claim, but it's quite another to back it up. Focus on something *precise* or *measurable* in the letter that will improve the client's quality of life or business prospects.

Examples of specific benefits include

- Incentive that adds value
- Research-tested growth in productivity
- No-risk terms of service
- Proven durability that reduces long-term costs
- Options tailored exclusively to the client's needs

Until you're prepared to identify each of these points, it's nearly impossible to begin writing effectively. So take the time now to sketch out the answers.

Note: Among the preceding questions, you'll find the first three covered in greater detail in this chapter; the final one is covered in Chapter 2.

FORMATTING

You're just about ready to open up a new document and get to work. Let's get the mechanics of printed letters out of the way first. This part isn't about writing per se, but it's no less vital to the image you're conveying.

The rules here are discussed within the framework of a printed letter. For special formatting rules regarding e-mails and text messages, see Chapter 4.

In the body of the letter, use 12-point type. Anything smaller is difficult to read, so don't cheat by dropping to 10-point type if you're trying to cram everything onto a single page. On the other end of the scale, anything that is larger than 12-point type looks awkward.

Paragraphs should be flush left, single-spaced. Some traditionalists like to indent new paragraphs without leaving space after each one, which is the method used in this book. While this works just fine for a denser, long-form work such as a book, it makes a letter tougher to read. For maximum reader-friendliness, keep some air between paragraphs by separating each one with a blank line.

If your letter is particularly short and you want to give the letter more gravity by filling out the page, set the line spacing to 1.5 lines.

In terms of typeface, you might peruse your word processing program's dozens of available fonts and be tempted to get creative with the actual look of the letter. Don't do it. Fancy, artistic typefaces may look great on wedding invitations, but they have no place in a sales letter. You want the letter to be professional and readable. I'm partial to Times New Roman for a classic, refined look or Arial for a clean, modern feel.

OPENING/SALUTATION

For a printed letter, this is the easiest part of all.

- Start with today's date on its own line.
- Add a blank line, and then stack the recipient's name, title, and address.
- Add a blank line, and start your salutation.
- Add another blank line, and start the letter.
- Make the type flush left—no need to indent anything.

With e-mails, you can skip everything before the salutation ("Dear Norma").

May 15, 20XX

Ms. Norma Smith
Client, Inc.
123 Main St., Suite 500
Anytown, NY 12345

Dear Norma:

[Body of letter starts here.]

Addressing the Reader

When was the last time you shook a client's hand and said, "Hello, Mr. Jones"? The days have long passed since business communication required that kind of stilted formality. In the salutation of your letter, you're almost always at liberty to greet your client by his or her first name regardless of whether you've actually met the person.

One key exception here is if your audience is extremely high-end or powerful, for example, CEOs, celebrities, or ultra-affluent consumers. They are accustomed to other people deferring to them on a regular basis, so your implied familiarity may rub them the wrong way. Maintain the proper distance, and stick to the old-fashioned "Dear Mr. Gates" or "Dear Ms. Winfrey."

Beyond that, you can use your judgment. If you've done enough background on your prospect to know that he or she is the stuffy type or if you perceive that the prospect far outstrips you in experience or stature, then you might want to err on the side of formality, at least in the first letter.

Mass Mailings

The preceding rule on addressing the reader applies even if you're sending out a mass mailing to hundreds of prospects. The worst thing you can do here is to fire off a blanket message with the catch-all salutation, "Dear Friend." It makes it painfully obvious to your prospect that he or she isn't your friend but is merely among the hordes of people getting the same pitch.

Instead, use a mailing database or e-mail distribution program (various software programs are available online) that allows you to personalize fields within the salutation and body of the message. Set up customization of the recipient's name in the salutation (again, first name only in most cases), and find a couple of spots within the text in which to drop the client's company name (if applicable).

If you're targeting businesses and your database includes job titles, try this trick: Drop in a sentence that says, "As <Job Title>, you understand how critical it is to. . . ." With the ability to drop in the recipient's actual title, this creates the perception that you're talking directly to that individual and not to a group.

A caveat: Be sure to run tests on these programs because they're certainly not infallible. Check as many letters as possible for quality control. If your client is Susan Jones at Dynamic Corp. and she receives a letter that begins "Dear Dynamic," you would have been better off addressing her as "Dear Friend."

If you don't have access to or funding for a customizable database, you'll have to tough it out and send the letter with no personalization. At the very least, try to address the recipients by their general profession or shared interests based on whatever level of information you have about them.

Dear Marketing Executive:
Dear Medical Professional:
Dear IT Decision Maker:
Dear Baseball Fan:
Dear Homeowner:

This establishes from the beginning that you know something essential about the person to whom you are writing and that the letter addresses his or her specific needs.

FIRST PARAGRAPH

So far, so good. Now comes the real work of the letter itself, which you can tackle by breaking down the message into its basic foundational parts. The first paragraph should present the problem or challenge that is faced by your client and then offer the general solution in the form of your product or service. Subsequent paragraphs should support the main point in more detail by describing specific client benefits, and the closing paragraph should let the reader know exactly what you want him or her to do.

Let's start by diagramming the opening paragraph—it's by far the most vital part of your letter, so you'll be spending the most time on it.

The Challenge . . . and the Solution

As a sales professional or entrepreneur, you are, by nature, a problem solver. Your organization has identified a need or gap in the marketplace and has filled it with a certain product or service. In other words, regardless of your actual offering, what you're really selling are *solutions*. So the logical way to start your letter is by stating the fundamental problem or need faced by your prospect.

Now, no one likes to be reminded about the personal or business challenges he or she faces—the gloom-and-doom approach doesn't get you very far with most people. So your task is to do it in a way that's compelling and attention-getting but at the same time empathetic and nonthreatening.

The next step? Solving the challenge, of course. Even before you dive into your product or service, you'll want to briefly describe how the prospect can optimize his or her situation. Here are a couple of ways to do this.

Business-to-Business Letter For a business-to-business letter, you might want to start by presenting the bigger picture of what's going on in the client's industry, followed by the general solution.

> You and I both know that the very nature of the widget industry is changing: Costs are rising, overseas competition is encroaching, and margins are being cut. In this challenging environment, the performance of your suppliers is critical.

In the following example, the solution is actually built into the setup sentence.

> In a competitive business environment where today's bright new idea is tomorrow's easily imitated commodity, speed to market is everything.

When you're reminding the prospect of a less-than-stellar situation in the marketplace, you'll want to frame it in as neutral a light as possible. Use phrases like *the industry is changing* instead of *the industry is in trouble*. Use words like *challenges* or *tests* instead of *problems* or *difficulties*.

If your prospect is fortunate enough to have things going swimmingly with his or her business or industry, acknowledge it, and then get the prospect thinking about what comes next.

> Congratulations to you and XYZ Corp. on a record-setting year for profits and revenue growth. You and I both know that challenges come with success: How can you maintain this solid performance, given that your competitors will come after you even harder? One answer is continual product innovation.

Consumer Letter When writing to a consumer prospect, the approach is a bit different. You might want to remind him or her about all the thinking that needs to go into making a key purchase decision. Then present the general solution.

> Finding the ideal new home certainly can be a challenge. You've got to think about mortgage costs, the quality of life in the neighborhood, your daily commute, and your space needs. Wouldn't you appreciate a real estate agent who brings you this information up front?

> With the volatile nature of today's securities markets, finding the right financial advisor is one of the most important decisions you'll make. Ask yourself whether your advisor has the experience, track record, and resources to help secure your financial future.

In the first example above, the solution is presented in the form of a rhetorical question. (See "Ask a Rhetorical Question" in Chapter 3 for more detail.) The latter example uses a modified version of the rhetorical question in which the challenge and the solution are inseparable. By getting prospects to ask themselves the question, you've helped them to arrive at the answer.

A slightly different approach is to build your letter around a seasonal theme or another hook that's timely and relevant to your prospect.

> If you're thinking about a fall wedding, it's time to start making plans for the big day. In just a few short months, you've got to pull together everything from catering to floral arrangements. Wouldn't it be great to have a pro on your side, one who has been creating dream weddings for years?

Again, before you can state the case for your product or service, you need to remind the reader of why he or she needs it.

The Core Idea

Now that you've set up the challenge and have offered a teaser solution, it's time for your product or service to swoop in on its white horse and rescue the prospect.

This is your *core idea*—the *one* thing you want the reader to remember from the letter. Yes, it's another way of describing that old business saw, the *unique selling point* (USP)—the specific claim that only your company can make and that sets you apart in the marketplace. To look at it another way, it's the written equivalent of the 30-second elevator pitch or the thesis statement from your college or grad-school writing days.

Since this is the crux of your message, don't skimp on the brainpower for this one or attempt to wing it. Put in as much time as necessary to build a compelling statement. Try out several options, and get opinions from colleagues or trusted business partners on which one makes the best case.

If you're brand new to the client, keep the core idea fairly general—if you get too granular, you'll have difficulty trying to support your idea in subsequent paragraphs. And make sure that you express your core idea either in the opening paragraph or in the opening sentence of the second paragraph. *Do not* begin the letter with a long, rambling treatise on the state of the industry, only to bury your lead halfway through the letter—the recipient may never get that far.

Here are a few examples of a core idea:

> XYZ Insurance Co. offers the most affordable, flexible life insurance policy choices in the industry.

> Acme, Inc., helps eco-conscious travelers have peace of mind on their vacations, knowing that every aspect of their trip is being carbon-offset.

> XYZ Diagnostic Co. sets the standard within the medical industry for advanced, exceptionally precise monitoring equipment and cost-effective operation.

> I offer a wide range of tax services targeted directly to small-business owners like you, at rates that fit a small-business budget.

Here's how the first core idea above might fit within an opening paragraph:

> Some of the most important questions are ones few of us want to address: Will my family be able to support itself when I'm gone? Can I afford to protect them when my budget is limited right now? XYZ Insurance Co. can help you deal with these issues in a stress-free way. We offer some of the most affordable, flexible life insurance policy choices in the industry.

Notice the flow: First comes the problem (my family might not be able to support itself in my absence; I'm not sure I can afford life insurance), then the solution (a stress-free way to deal with those issues), and then your core idea (XYZ's life insurance policies are flexible and affordable).

Also notice that when it is dropped into the paragraph, the core idea is altered slightly from the original stand-alone version (in this case so that the company's name falls in the preceding sentence).

No matter; the basic idea hasn't changed. You're allowed to tweak it a bit to fit into the context of the paragraph.

Here's one more example of a core idea:

> Acme Corp. manufactures the highest-quality industrial tools, designed to help keep your operations running smoothly and efficiently.

And here's how it might fit within an opening paragraph:

> With operational costs rising in the widget industry, now is the ideal time to reassess the effectiveness of your existing manufacturing tools. One supplier has your long-term needs in mind: Acme Corp. We manufacture the highest-quality industrial tools, designed to help keep your operations running smoothly and efficiently.

Again, notice the flow: First comes the problem (operational costs are rising), then the solution (time to reassess your tools), and then your core idea (Acme Corp.'s tools keep operations running smoothly and efficiently). The original core idea again has been altered slightly, placing the company's name in the preceding sentence.

The Core Idea in Follow-up Letters

If your letter is a follow-up note rather than an introductory letter, you can more or less skip the whole problem/solution setup. Instead, go right to the core idea. Rather than repeating every point from the original letter, though, start to get more precise. Lead with a more focused core idea that's relevant to this new stage of the sales process, and stick to it throughout the letter.

Later in this book, in Chapter 5, you'll find much more on how to handle specific situations throughout the entire sales process.

SUPPORTING PARAGRAPHS

Everything you write after the first paragraph should reinforce the core idea. Period. It's vital that you express your idea in more detail because no one will buy your sales claim without adequate proof. As you craft your letter, think about two or three *specific* or *measurable* points that will support your central argument.

By *specific*, I mean something that ideally can be quantified. If you're claiming to help make a client's customer-service operation more efficient, make sure that you've got data in your back pocket to demonstrate how the typical call time can be reduced, for example. Or be able to produce a case study about how you improved efficiency for another client.

By *measurable*, I mean something that ideally can be verified by an objective source outside your organization. If possible, find and use whatever independent research, industry awards, or press coverage that can support your claim.

Even if it's general data about your industry or product category—and not necessarily about you or your company—you can let some of that authority rub off on your brand. For example, if you're selling hybrid vehicles but your particular vehicle isn't the most efficient model in its class, you can elevate it by quoting a study on hybrids in general: "The latest research reveals that, on average, hybrid vehicles deliver 20 percent higher fuel economy than nonhybrids." Yours might be only, say, 15 percent higher, but you haven't made any claims about its actual performance, have you?

On this note, remember that this exercise isn't necessarily about superlatives. You don't need to make claims that your product or service is the "best" this or the "fastest" that, even if you can back them up. Your clients know as well as you that statistics aren't necessarily the last word—they can be "spun" to whatever advantage you choose.

If your sales claims lean to the more humble or conservative side, you have less of a burden of proof, but you still need to give some evidence. For example, if you state, "We're a family business, so we value customer relationships above all else," you should support it by briefly describing the loyalty your family has shown to the community over the years and by throwing in a glowing testimonial or two from clients.

If you're brand new to the field or your company is a pure startup, the odds are that you have very little to go on: no client case studies, no press mentions, and scant research. In this case, take your experience from other fields or endeavors, and use it to your advantage: "I've delivered solid productivity gains for clients in the widget field. . . . Now I'm putting this proven track record to work for you in the thingamajig industry." Then present examples of your accomplishments and how they relate to your current offering.

Now let's go back and look at one of the core idea examples presented in the preceding section and line up some supporting points to make the case.

The core idea:

> Acme Corp. manufactures the highest-quality industrial tools, designed to help keep your operations running smoothly and efficiently.

Supporting point 1:

> Acme Corp. tools are made of high-strength, lightweight titanium—the most durable, advanced material found in the industry.

This supports the "highest quality" claim in the core idea. (Note that you're not claiming that you're the *only* company to use titanium, just that the material is the best in the field.) Ideally, you would need a third party to prove that none of your competitors use a newer or more durable material; your best bet is to quote from one of the industry trade journals, if possible.

Supporting point 2:

> A leading study has proven that companies using Acme Corp. tools have increased manufacturing speed and capacity by an average of 10%.

This supports the point about efficiency. Be prepared to reveal the sourcing behind that study, even if it was commissioned internally by your company.

Supporting point 3:

> The Acme Corp. comprehensive service plan helps to ensure worry-free operations over the long term.

This supports the point about smooth operation. No need for independent verification; just be ready to lay out that plan in some detail when the time comes and show the client exactly how it makes his or her life easier.

Each of the preceding supporting points should be highlighted in their own individual paragraphs following the core idea. They don't necessarily need to be the first sentence in their respective paragraphs, but you'll want to get to them no later than the second sentence.

Then, depending on how much depth you want to get into (*recommendation:* not too much, especially in a cold-call introductory note), you can fill out the rest of the paragraph with material that backs up the supporting point.

Here is an example of a full paragraph incorporating supporting point 1:

> When you work with us, you invest in quality. Acme Corp. tools are made of high-strength, lightweight titanium—the most durable, advanced
>
> *continued on next page*

> material found in the industry. *Widget Journal* calls titanium "the state of the art in the field and a revolutionary advance that will help to lower long-term manufacturing costs."

Here is an example of a full paragraph incorporating supporting point 2:

> This kind of quality produces measurable results. In fact, an independent study by Whatsit Research Co. has proven that companies using our products have increased their manufacturing speed and capacity by an average of 10%. For a midsize company like yours, this translates into cost savings of up to $3 million a year. In a competitive market, it's the ultimate advantage.

Note that in this paragraph incorporating supporting point 2, the original supporting point has been adjusted slightly to fit the context of the paragraph. Also note the transition ("This kind of quality . . .") that bridges the first supporting paragraph with the second.

Here is an example of a full paragraph incorporating supporting point 3:

> Your investment is backed by Acme's comprehensive service plan, which helps to ensure worry-free operation over the long term. You'll get technical support that covers maintenance for up to five years—so you can focus on running your business without getting hit by unexpected repair costs.

Again, the supporting point has been altered a bit to smooth the transition from the preceding paragraph.

Using the preceding guidelines, spend a couple of minutes sketching out a quick outline including your client's challenge and your main point, followed by supporting paragraphs and their main points. And to recap, you might want to start digging up the following pieces of information to demonstrate your specific or measurable claims:

- Third-party or internal research
- Trade or consumer press mentions
- Industry awards
- Client case studies or testimonials
- Past performance results from your other business experiences

CALL TO ACTION

The most productive sales calls or customer meetings are those that end with you asking your client to *do* something—get more information, get a pricing estimate, or sign the contract. Sales letters are no different.

Close your note by telling the reader exactly what you what him or her to do. Unless you're comfortable making a hyperaggressive opening pitch, this doesn't necessarily mean making the "ask" or the hard close. That most likely comes after you've had face-to-face or phone contact with the client (techniques for the sales close are discussed in Chapter 5).

For now, your goal should be to get some kind of positive, personal reaction to your letter. Even if you state that you will call to set up an appointment, you still should ask something of the prospect.

Using the industrial tooling example presented earlier, here are a couple of ways to wrap up the introductory note:

> Please take a look at our latest sales brochure, which I've included here. You'll find that Acme Corp. offers a wealth of industrial tooling solutions that can enhance productivity and save money. For more information, feel free to contact me at . . .

> As you begin to review your company's operations budget, please consider Acme Corp. tools as a vital asset that will help you to increase productivity and save money. I will follow up with you via e-mail in the next few days. In the meantime, if you have any questions, feel free to contact me at . . .

Note that key selling points are reinforced in the call to action—it's your final opportunity to drive home your message. (It's best not to repeat the selling points verbatim. Add a little variety to the language, but stay on message.) Also note the use of the word *please*. Politeness and respect are always appreciated.

More assertive sales pros and entrepreneurs likely will opt for the proactive approach taken in the last example—that you'll follow up with the prospect, not the other way around. (If it's your standard practice to follow up on the phone or via e-mail with your prospects, then say so in the letter so that it doesn't come as a surprise.)

When you tell the prospect that you will follow up, it's best not to make a self-serving statement—no prospect wants to be reminded that he or she is about to get a sales pitch on the phone. Instead, give the perception that you want to brainstorm, strategize, or discuss some ideas about helping the prospect with his or her business challenge.

Instead of

> I will follow up in the next week to discuss how XYZ, Inc.'s solutions can work for your company.

try

> I will follow up in the next week to brainstorm some ideas on how your company can best meet the challenges of rapidly expanding global competition.

Finally, it's never a bad idea to thank the prospect (by name) for his or her time and sneak in what's called an *assumed close*—meaning that you just *know* the two of you will be doing business soon.

> Thanks for reading, Sally—I look forward to helping you find answers to your insurance needs.

For more on personalizing the letter, see "Personalize It" in Chapter 3. For more on the assumed close, see "Be Confident," also in Chapter 3.

CLOSING

It's your call as to how you want to sign off. I am partial to "Best regards" or just "Best," but feel free to use the tried-and-true "Sincerely." (I've always found "Sincerely yours" and "Cordially yours" to be a bit much. After all, are you really *theirs*?)

Even if you're sending an e-mail with a standard, automatic "signature" at the bottom of the message (including your name, title, company, and contact information) or if your printed stationery includes this same information, use both your first and last names in the sign-off. You can shift to use of your first name only once you've established rapport with the client.

If you're mailing a copy of the letter to one or more of the prospect's colleagues, include a "cc" line. It's acceptable to use an initial for the person's first name.

cc: D. Jones
       P. Smith

Finally, if you've included an attachment with the letter, add the word *enclosure* (or the abbreviation *encl.*) on the last line of the letter.

ENVELOPE

I won't dwell too much on the topic of envelopes because it falls outside the realm of the writing process, but if you're going to mail or hand deliver a printed message, keep it simple. If your company logo and address aren't printed directly on the envelope, use a return address label. (Some companies, citing security concerns, won't even accept a letter or package without a return address.) Don't hand write the recipient's information; print it on a label or on the envelope itself.

And unless you're selling nuclear secrets, don't try to get coy and stamp the envelope "Personal" or "Confidential" in the hope that it will get the recipient to open it. It's an old direct-mail trick, and it raises expectations that likely will annoy your prospect when he or she sees it's a sales pitch.

Letter-Perfect Rules

Let's continue the analogy that your letter or e-mail is like a sculpture carved from stone. You've now chipped away at enough material to block out the basic form. Your core idea, supporting points, and call to action are in place, and now you can begin to see the rough parameters of your creation. This chapter will present tips on how to start carving out the features that will bring your work to life—and get it read from start to finish.

1. KEEP IT SIMPLE

As much as you love your company and know every nuance about its operations, the truth is that most people have neither the time nor the desire to hear you ramble on about it. So keep a tight focus. If you try to write a manifesto that includes your company's entire story, the recipient will tune out pretty quickly. Even if you think that you can cram it all into a single page, resist the urge. At its best, the sales letter should whet a client's appetite for more information.

The key is to prioritize based on your core idea, as discussed in Chapter 1. You've already identified two or three main sales points, and you have only so much real estate in which to bring them to life.

When plotting your letter, you might want to first grab a separate sheet of paper and sketch out a table with two or three columns representing your main sales points. Underneath each point, add any available information that you feel will serve to support the point. Such information could include

- Company legacy/history/community involvement
- Company growth
- Company values
- Case studies of positive client experiences
- Overview of product line
- Overview of services
- News about product launches

- Product firsts or innovative practices
- Independent or corporate-commissioned research
- Client testimonials
- Press mentions
- Special pricing/offers
- Service guarantees
- Professional experience (yours or the company principals')
- Socially responsible business practices

Set these items in priority order within each column of your planning table. (In other words, determine which items best support the sales points.) In your actual letter, use only the first one or two items per main point. Keep the rest in your pocket for future correspondence, when you start to narrow down the message based on your client's needs and how the negotiation is proceeding.

When you consider how much there is to say about your product or service, you'll quickly realize that there's no way to do it all in a single letter. This exercise helps to bring some necessary discipline to the message.

2. KEEP IT BRIEF

It would follow, then, that simplicity equals brevity. The most precious commodity your prospects own is their time. Respect it.

You should be able to replicate the experience of a persuasive face-to-face sales call in just a few paragraphs. Unless you're far along in the sales process and you're starting to get into complex, detailed discussions about product specs or pricing—in which case your letter is really more of a proposal—avoid writing letters of more than one page in length. For e-mail, this is the equivalent of six or seven brief paragraphs.

Self-editing may be the toughest part of the letter-writing process. If you find that your letter is spilling onto a second page or if your e-mail is bloating into 10 paragraphs, go back and look carefully for passages in which you can trim the fat. You'll be surprised at how many nonessential clauses or bits of tangential language you'll find.

In Chapter 6 you'll find some examples of redundant language—common instances in which writers use four or five words to say something when they could say it more effectively using one or two. Purge your letter of these redundancies and other kinds of excess. If you find it too difficult to self-edit, ask a colleague to take a crack at it.

The Concise Opener

To maximize the impact of your core idea, keep the first sentence brief. (You even might try crafting a one-sentence opening paragraph; it's a good opportunity to grab the reader's attention.)

Here's an example of a concise, single-sentence opening paragraph:

> In a marketplace where the best idea wins, you deserve an R&D partner with the experience to make products market-ready—which is exactly what XYZ Corp. brings to its clients.

After that, use a variety of paragraph lengths, if possible, to keep things interesting. While some supporting points require more explanation than others, try to avoid writing paragraphs of more than 125 words or so.

3. ASK, WHAT'S IN IT FOR MY CLIENT?

So now you've got a concise, tightly focused letter with a well-defined core idea, two or three main supporting points, and one or two specific pieces of evidence reinforcing each point. Done, right? Well, not just yet.

Your sales claims can't be allowed to just float in a vacuum. Where feasible, each point in the letter should be tethered to a specific benefit for your client. Apply the "so what" test to each statement. Ask yourself whether anyone cares about something like this:

> XYZ Corp. recently received a major honor from the Widget Trade Commission.

Hey, that plaque probably looks fantastic on your wall. But so what? How does it benefit the *customer*? How about

> XYZ Company's recent honor from the Widget Trade Commission means that you're getting a product endorsed by the leaders of the industry.

Instead of

> We've been serving the widget industry for more than 50 years.

try

> We've been serving the widget industry for more than 50 years. Our experience ensures that you're getting a proven partner with trusted service.

Now, making these connections throughout the letter might seem awkward (e.g., "Our software is scalable. This benefits you because . . ." or, "Our new condo properties are centrally located. This benefits you because . . ."). The key is to do it subtly, in just a few words.

> Our software is scalable, so no matter how much your company grows, you'll have a solution that continues to meet your needs.

> Thanks to the central location of our properties, you've got an easy 12-minute commute to downtown and the shopping district.

Make an Emotional Appeal

You can take the client benefit a step further by delving deep into your customer's *real* motivation for buying. Consider for a moment why we buy anything. Our logical, rational side wants to believe that it has control over the decision, which is why we attempt to justify our purchases by citing facts, statistics, and other quantifiable factors ("I bought that sports car because it received the highest ranking in the owner-satisfaction survey").

The truth is, however, that we buy for raw, emotional, gut-level reasons ("Okay, I really bought that car because I want to look good at the high school reunion").

You can get to the heart of a customer's purchase motivation by subtly appealing to the core emotional benefit. If you can help a prospect imagine how he or she will *feel* after making the purchase decision, you're a step further down the road to making the sale.

To expand on a couple of earlier examples, here's how you can bring in the emotional element:

> Our software is scalable, so no matter how much your company grows, you'll have a solution that continues to meet your needs—along with employees who are grateful for the smooth upgrades.

> Thanks to the central location of our properties, you've got an easy 12-minute commute to downtown and the shopping district—giving you more time to spend on what you really enjoy in life.

4. BE PROFESSIONAL

Your written voice is just as important to the effectiveness of your sales pitch as your speaking voice. While you're writing, try this simple test: Read the letter aloud. If it doesn't plausibly sound like you're having a conversation with the client over the phone, then you're not using the right tone.

Keep it friendly, professional, and conversational. Ideally, you want to split the difference between sounding like someone with whom the reader could become friends and someone with whom he or she could easily do business.

Of course, you'll want to be able to "talk the talk" of your prospect's business—demonstrating your depth of knowledge in the field. If you're writing to doctors, you'll need to prove your dexterity with complex medical language. If you're writing to Web developers, you'll have to navigate programming lingo comfortably. But don't go overboard. Limit any jargon to the terms necessary to describe the specific product or service. As I mentioned in the introduction, people want to be spoken to as human beings regardless of their insider status.

You don't want to sound too academic and stuffy—it usually translates as fake or condescending, and you'll probably lull the reader to sleep before the second paragraph. Using long, convoluted sentences and four-syllable words won't get you very far with most audiences.

Neither do you want to come off like the overly aggressive hawker who's just guzzled three cans of Red Bull—your pitch again will seem insincere, and you'll just sound inexperienced. Too many businesspeople allow their writing to drift in this direction without even realizing it. This is so because they attempt to use excessive type formatting as a way to communicate urgency or importance.

Try to keep this impulse in check. Avoid riddling your letter with cheap, attention-getting ploys such as these:

- **Large sections of boldface type**
- EXCESSIVE USE OF UPPERCASE TYPE
- Lots of exclamation points!!!!!
- Multiple question marks ("Doesn't this sound like a great deal???")

Otherwise, you might as well be shouting at your client. And no one likes to be shouted at. (See rule 7 for more clarification on when and how to use bold or italic type.)

By the way, doing *any* kind of type formatting in an e-mail is especially pointless (see Chapter 4 for more details).

5. GRAB ATTENTION WITH A HEADLINE

When you see a particularly interesting print ad, what's the first thing you notice other than an arresting photo or image? The headline—especially if it features a clever use of language.

A headline can have the same impact when used in your letters—it is, in fact, usually the most noticeable element of a sales note. But you should use one only if you have something truly compelling to say. (With e-mails, there's no need to include a headline within the body of the e-mail because e-mails have a subject line.)

Try to avoid using a headline just for the sake of plastering a generic statement across the top of the page.

> **XYZ's New Payroll Technology Is Truly Exciting!**

Who cares? Instead, use a headline if, for example, you've got a product release or a new development that will benefit the customer directly—and you have some specific piece of evidence to back it up.

> **Save Up to 40% in Payroll Costs with XYZ's Payroll3000**

Or, if you're kicking off your letter with a client case study, the headline could serve as a teaser for the story to follow.

> **One of Our Fortune 500 Clients Needed a Payroll Solution . . . Fast**

(See Chapter 3 for more information about how to lead with a client case study.)

Another good headline device is to use a testimonial or endorsement quote about your product from a customer or from the consumer or trade press.

> **Widget Press: XYZ's Payroll3000 Is "Revolutionary"**

Finally, think back to the structure of your opening paragraph. The first thing you need to do in a letter is to establish the prospect's business or personal challenge and then offer the solution. A hard-hitting headline can do both. Thus, when the letter starts, you can move more quickly to a discussion of your own services. Here's one example:

> **Wouldn't You Jump at a Chance to Turn Back Rising Payroll Costs?**

Regardless of the hook you decide to use, keep it brief—12 words or less, if possible. If the headline spills onto a second line, cut it back.

To enhance the impact of the headline, bump up the type size to 14 or 16 points, in bold. Avoid making it all caps because that's too over the top. I like to center it, but you can make it flush left if that's your preference. In terms of placement, it should go directly above the salutation.

6. BREAK IT UP WITH SUBHEADS

Within the body of your letter, you can provide some visual relief by using bold subheads. They act as markers for your main sales points—if the prospect gives your letter a cursory 10-second glance, these are the words he or she most likely will remember.

Use subheads to divide clearly defined sections within the letter. The logical way to do this is to employ them as introductions to each supporting paragraph.

Going back to the example from the "Supporting Paragraphs" section of Chapter 1, here's how subheads might work throughout a letter, starting with the core idea (sections condensed):

Acme Corp. manufactures the highest-quality industrial tools, designed to help keep your operations running smoothly and efficiently.

Innovative Materials Built to Last

When you work with us, you invest in quality. Acme Corp. tools are made of high-strength, lightweight titanium—the most durable, advanced material found in the industry. *Widget Journal* calls titanium "the state of the art in the field."

Better Efficiency, Greater Cost Savings

This kind of quality produces measurable results. In fact, an independent study by Whatsit Research Co. has proven that companies using our products have increased their manufacturing speed and capacity by an average of 10%. . . .

A Stress-Free Service Plan

Your investment is backed by Acme's comprehensive service plan, which helps to ensure worry-free operation over the long term. You'll get technical support that covers maintenance for up to five years—so you can focus on running your business. . . .

Note that the subheads here summarize and rephrase the points made in the letter—a subhead shouldn't be a verbatim duplicate of text from the paragraph that follows it. Try to maintain the same construction among the subheads. The preceding examples all start with *things*—innovative materials, better efficiency, and a stress-free plan. This makes it easier for the prospect to grasp if he or she is skimming the letter.

Subheads should be even shorter than a headline—ideally, eight words or less. Make them bold type; centering is optional. Using body-text size (12 points) is fine.

If you can't decide whether to use subheads, keep in mind this tradeoff: While they help to make your letter more readable and memorable, they also add length to the message. By keeping your writing concise and absorbing within a single page, you may not need them.

7. MAKE THE CONNECTIONS

The best sales letters aren't merely a collection of sales points and a call to action. They tell a story that flows from beginning to end. Thus, when you leave one sales point and move to another, don't just grind the gears and lurch forward. Make it a smooth transition, and give the reader the sense that each point is inseparable from the others.

To create this perception, you can employ simple phrases that help you to make the connection: *it begins with, because of, thanks to, together, this adds up to, this translates into.* Such phrases contribute greatly to a coherent, logical message.

Using the sample paragraphs from the preceding section minus the subheads, here's how you could incorporate transitions among the key points (transition terms are shown below in boldface type for emphasis):

> Acme Corp. manufactures the highest-quality industrial tools, designed to help keep your operations running smoothly and efficiently.
>
> **The quality of our tools begins with** their materials: Acme Corp. tools are made of high-strength, lightweight titanium, which is the most

durable, advanced material found in the industry. *Widget Journal* calls titanium "the state of the art in the field."

This kind of quality produces measurable results. In fact, an independent study by Whatsit Research Co. has proven that companies using our products have increased their manufacturing speed and capacity by an average of 10%. For a midsize company like yours, this translates into cost savings of up to $3 million a year. In a competitive market, it's the ultimate advantage.

Your investment in quality and efficiency is backed by Acme's comprehensive service plan, which helps to ensure worry-free operation over the long term. You'll get technical support that covers maintenance for up to five years—so you can focus on running your business without getting hit by unexpected repair costs.

These benefits add up to an industrial tooling solution that can keep your company competitive in the long run. Please take a look at our enclosed brochure . . .

8. FRAME IT WITH BULLET POINTS

Bullets are a good device for summarizing features or benefits. They represent another effective way to provide visual relief, allowing your reader to catch some of your key points at a glance.

Once you've completed the first draft of your letter, go back and look at each paragraph. Is there a spot where you're presenting a long laundry list of features or benefits? Few customers will want to wade through it. Instead, try reformatting the list as bullet points.

Too long:

> XYZ Insurance offers medical insurance plans with leading features, including low premiums, reduced co-pays, low-cost prescription drug coverage, a large provider network, 24-hour customer service, and substantial dental and vision benefits.

Better:

> XYZ Insurance offers medical insurance plans with leading features, including
>
> - Low premiums
> - Reduced co-pays
> - Low-cost prescription drug coverage
> - A large provider network
> - 24-hour customer service
> - Substantial dental and vision benefits

Make sure that the bulleted items don't become paragraphs in their own right—try to limit each one to a few words. Additionally, try to keep each bullet point around the same length. If one bullet is 20 words long and the rest are three, the list looks strange.

As with subheads, maintain the same construction throughout. Your bullets should either be a list of items, as above, or action verbs, as below:

With XYZ Insurance, you'll have a key opportunity to

- Lower your premiums
- Reduce your co-pays
- Access low-cost prescription drug coverage
- Choose from a large provider network
- Contact 24-hour customer service
- Enjoy substantial dental and vision benefits

Again, the rule is: *Use in moderation*. Avoid placing more than one bullet-point list in your letter. And because they occupy a significant amount of vertical space, try to keep bullet-point lists to six lines or less—you can use tabs or column formatting to arrange short bullet items in two columns if necessary.

Formatting

Use simple round or square bullets only. Unusually shaped symbols (checkmarks, stars, etc.) may draw attention to that portion of the letter, but they often look amateurish. And be careful about attempting to format bullets within e-mails. You're better off using simple dashes or asterisks to indicate each new item.

9. USE BOLD AND ITALIC TYPE SPARINGLY

Italics should be used mainly for their traditional purpose: for magazine, news-paper, book, and movie titles. However, they can be employed within limits for emphasis. Use a well-placed italic word or short phrase if it's a real zinger that will have some kind of emotional impact—but don't italicize a full sentence. Here's an example of where italics help to drive home a solution:

> Configuration management costs have been skyrocketing. With our software, however, you can actually *lower* those costs by as much as 25%.

Boldface type also should be used only occasionally. If you're going to use it at all, limit it to items such as headlines, special features, or benefits that have formal names.

Do not use boldface type as a tool to draw attention to random words—this goes back to the point about sounding professional. If you're mentioning your company's name only a few times in the letter, it's okay to boldface the name each time. However, if you mention the name 20 times on one page, forget the boldface type altogether.

Bad use of type formatting:

> **XYZ Corp.** has been *in business for over 25 years,* so you can be assured that you're getting the **most polished, professional service.** At **XYZ Corp.,** our employees have been trained to provide **top-notch customer care.** Each one follows the **XYZ Corp.** credo: Treat *customers* the way we'd like to be treated.

Better use of type formatting:

> At **XYZ Corp.,** we're serious about customer care. According to *Widget Monthly,* our service options are "the best in the business." Here's a small sampling of plan options:
>
> *continued on next page*

- **Gold**—our premier customer program, including 24-hour personalized service
- **Silver**—our most popular plan, offering preset support during your busy periods
- **Bronze**—our most affordable plan, with pay-as-you-go service

The same rule applies to underlining. In fact, underlining appears so disruptive within the body of a letter that I'd recommend against using it at all.

Regarding e-mail, the rule again is to avoid all attempts at type formatting. See Chapter 4 for details.

10. LEAVE THEM WITH A P.S.

The postscript (P.S.) is the third-most-read portion of letters—after the headline and first sentence. A good postscript is the equivalent of making a strong, persuasive case with someone in conversation and then, just as you're about to walk away, turning back and saying, "Oh, there's one more thing. . . ."

So when do you use one? It's a strong device when you want to

- Highlight one of your earlier selling points (just make sure that you rephrase it—don't just copy and paste an earlier phrase)
- Briefly mention a new sales point—one that doesn't require a long explanation
- Add some variety to your letters if you're sending regular correspondence to one person

If at all possible, try to sneak in another mention of the call to action. In general, though, keep the postscript brief—anything more than two sentences will make it seem as though you don't know how to end the letter.

Here are a couple of examples of highlighting a point made earlier in the letter (emphasis added for illustration):

P.S.: *Just a reminder* that if you sign up by March 30, we'll extend your plan by one month, absolutely free of charge. Take care of it now by calling me at 123-555-1212, and enjoy the savings later.

P.S.: *Remember*, 8 in 10 customers of XYZZ Corp. refer us to others. To learn more about how you can enjoy this industry-leading customer service, visit our Web site at www.xyzzcorp-1.com.

Here are a couple of examples introducing a new sales point or offer (emphasis added for illustration):

P.S.: *Did you know that* by choosing Acme Widgets, you'll get the industry's best warranty? Call me at 123-555-1212 to enjoy worry-free ownership with three-year, all-inclusive coverage.

P.S.: *One more reason* to try us: If you register online at www.xyzz corp-1.com by November 30, you'll get a discount of 50% on your first month of service. A cost-effective solution just got even better.

Chapter 3

Deal-Makers

Solid organization makes your letter more practical and understandable; proper form makes it more professional. But these two items are only a fraction of what it takes to craft a strong sales letter or e-mail. It's time to add the finer details that get a "Sold" sticker placed next to your sculpture at the local gallery. To do so you'll need to reach deep into the writer's toolkit and get creative in your approach.

Welcome to what I call *deal-makers*. These small, almost imperceptible techniques and devices can help you to get from point *A* to point *B*—from your initial contact in writing to the close of the deal—as quickly and efficiently as possible.

Many of the methods described in this chapter are modern variations on principles established by the legends of direct marketing—those who have taken a scientific approach to the art of persuasion. The techniques presented here are not just best guesses about what works. Through countless trials and comparative testing of specific words and phrases, they have been proven to generate impressive levels of response.

From this vast store of information, I've selected what I feel are the most effective, easy-to-implement tips. Until they become second nature to you, here's the best way to put them into action: Start by writing your sales note in the most straightforward, structurally sound way possible, as addressed earlier in this book. Next, identify a handful of opportunities to finely hone the language—places where a riveting turn of phrase will really get your prospect thinking about his or her needs and how your product or service fulfills them. Then start sharpening.

Avoid the temptation to stuff a single letter full of these techniques. The devices are subtly influential when used individually, but when clumsily bunched together sentence after sentence, they can make a letter unreadable. As with everything else, it's all about moderation.

Just as important to this chapter are the concepts that *aren't* included. I've left out certain tried-and-true principles from the direct-marketing canon because some of them, quite frankly, have lost their relevance to modern audiences.

For example, some old-school direct-marketing books tell you to open your letters with wide-eyed enthusiasm ("I just couldn't wait to tell you about this great opportunity for your business!") or with an overly earnest plea ("May I have just five minutes of your time to tell you about an idea that will improve your life?"). Others resort to cliché when demonstrating a call to action ("What have you got to lose? Sign up today!").

Do people really talk like this? And if they did, would you want to listen to them? Remember the phone rule: If you can't plausibly read your letter to someone over the phone, you're using the wrong tone.

Many of the direct-marketing guides also suggest that you load up your letters with the hot-button words that trigger supposedly surefire emotional responses: *Bonus! New! Better! Free!* I'm not asking you to ignore words such as these; they're an important part of your message, and in many cases are virtually impossible to avoid. To highlight them in capital letters or hammer them over and over again, however, in service of transparent sales hyperbole is to lose a measure of credibility with your audience.

You can sell or persuade just as effectively without hitting people over the head. Today's consumer and business-to-business crowds are savvier than ever when it comes to marketing, and they're far more likely to tune out if they realize they're on the wrong end of a blatant pitch. These days it's about *conversation marketing*—building the perception of an authentic two-way dialogue between you and the prospect.

With that, let's get back to your work in progress. It's time to break out the chisel and give it the finishing touches.

GIVE THEM THE "I"

Unless you're a sole proprietor or a true independent contractor such as a licensed real estate or insurance agent, the odds are that you're representing an organization larger than yourself. So your general frame of reference in letters is *we* ("We deliver . . .") and *our* ("Our products are . . .").

But are there times when you can achieve greater impact by separating yourself from the organization you represent? Yes, near the beginning and close of the letter. Using the first-person voice in these spots establishes that there's a human being behind the logo on the letterhead and gives you an opening for connecting later on the phone or in person. After all, people want to deal with other people, not faceless corporate entities.

Once you've stated the client's challenge and your core solution, bring yourself into the equation. Using the opening-paragraph example from Chapter 1, here's how you might lead into a personal introduction:

> Dear Stan:
>
> With operational costs rising in the widget industry, now is the ideal time to reassess the effectiveness of your existing manufacturing tools. One company has your long-term needs in mind: Acme Corp. We manufacture the highest-quality industrial tools, designed to help keep your operations running smoothly and efficiently.
>
> I'm writing today to give you some inside knowledge about what Acme is doing to help companies like yours. For example, Acme tools are delivering measurable results. . . .

Then, after going through the features and benefits of your products or services in the supporting paragraphs, you can bring yourself back in as part of the call to action. Here's an example based on a passage used in Chapter 1:

> As you begin to review your company's operations budget, I'd like you to strongly consider Acme Corp. tools as an asset that will help you to increase productivity and save money. I will follow up with you via e-mail in the next few days. In the meantime, if you have any questions, please feel free to contact me at . . .

USE AN ACTIVE VOICE

Verb constructions such as *can be found, has been discovered,* or *is being presented* are not only clumsy, but they also flatten the impact of your letter and add unnecessary distance between you and the reader. Instead, use simple, active verbs to boost your message.

Instead of

> Durability, strength, and award-winning quality can be found in Acme Corp. fitness products.

try

> You'll find durability, strength, and award-winning quality in Acme Corp. fitness products.

Instead of

> A strong investment has been made by Acme Corp. in the research and development of all its products.

try

> Acme Corp. has made a strong investment in the research and development of all its products.

Instead of

> This leads to a significant reduction in call-center response time.

try

> This significantly lowers call-center response time.

DON'T JUST PROVIDE; DELIVER

Write enough sales letters and you'll find yourself getting sick of two verbs: *provide* and *offer*. When describing your company's products or services, it's easy to fall into the pattern of using these words again and again ("We provide a high level of service. . . ." "Our company offers an exclusive product. . . ."). But you'd do well to substitute those verbs occasionally with ones that are more action-oriented. This simple step makes your company seem more dynamic and customer-driven.

Examples (shown in italics for emphasis) include

Acme Corp. *delivers* award-winning customer service. . . .

XYZ Corp. *produces* an extensive line of customizable widgets. . . .

This year, Acme Corp. will *put forth* its most advanced system yet. . . .

XYZ Corp. *generates* more than $20 million in small-business loans each year. . . .

Acme Corp. *affords* its customers the opportunity to switch plans at any time. . . .

XYZ Corp. *contributes* in many ways to the success of its clients. . . .

If you're going to use *offer* in the sense of making a formal sales offer, you can add a bit more weight by preceding it with the phrase *prepared* to.

We're *prepared* to *offer* a two-year contract for $100,000.

This doesn't work so well with *provide* (*prepared to provide* is a bit awkward). And it's overkill if you use it more than once in a letter.

FOCUS ON THE READER'S VIEWPOINT

Don't automatically make your company the subject of the sentence, even when referring to the benefits and advantages you deliver. It sounds a little self-serving and doesn't convey empathy. Flip the focus so that at least one or two sentences capture your client's perspective.

Instead of constantly leading with yourself or your company, as in a sentence such as

> We offer an extensive package of software solutions, helping clients to achieve their productivity goals.

try turning it around:

> You can achieve your productivity goals through our extensive suite of software solutions.

Instead of

> XYZ Corp. provides the most flexible, affordable telecom services for small businesses.

try

> A small business like yours demands the most flexible, affordable telecom services—the kind you'll get from XYZ Corp.

Instead of

> As a financial advisor with over 20 years of experience, I can leverage my expertise to help you plan for retirement.

try

> As you plan for retirement, you'll have the advantage of working with an expert financial advisor who has over 20 years of experience.

It sometimes may require a bit more verbiage to achieve the effect, but it's worth it to make a more direct appeal.

Note: If you use the second-person structure exclusively throughout the letter ("You will benefit from . . ." or "Your company will gain . . ."), things can get monotonous pretty quickly, just as they would if you focus on yourself or your company throughout. As with every other deal-makers tip, use sparingly.

ASK A RHETORICAL QUESTION

Let's play *Jeopardy!* Sometimes you can make a more effective point by phrasing it in the form of a question. I'm talking specifically about the *rhetorical* question—

the type of question that's actually a declarative statement and for which no real answer is required or expected.

Instead of

> As your real estate agent, I'll work tirelessly on your behalf until you find the home of your dreams. This is the kind of commitment you want from a real estate professional.

try

> As your real estate agent, I'll work tirelessly on your behalf until you find the home of your dreams. Isn't that the kind of commitment you want from a real estate professional?

Instead of

> Don't settle for a cookie-cutter approach to investment vehicles, as offered by most financial advisors.

try

> Most financial advisors offer a cookie-cutter approach to investment vehicles. But why would you want to settle for that?

Instead of

> Our solution has helped other industry leaders reduce time to market, boost quality control, and minimize expenses.

try

> If you knew that other industry leaders use a solution that reduces time to market, boosts quality control, and minimizes expenses, wouldn't you want to take advantage of it?

You know the answers to these questions, of course, and so do your prospects. By simply asking them, you'll get your prospects to frame their decision making the way you want them to.

LOOK FOR COMMON GROUND

Call this the "I feel your pain" school of letter writing. Put yourself in the company of the prospect, telling him or her, in effect, "I know your business. I know your priorities. We're in the same boat."

> As independent contractors, both you and I are faced with the challenge of finding affordable health care.

> As technology professionals, both you and I have to deal with the challenge of fast-growing server needs.

> As service-based executives working through an unpredictable economic period, you and I both benefit from generating added value for our clients.

Note: Always use *you and I* rather than *we*. The former sounds more intimate and personal, whereas with the latter, it's unclear to the prospect whether you mean the two of you or if you're using *we* to refer to your company.

This device is a good way to kick off the letter, as an alternative to a traditional opening. (It's also a different take on the "Give Them the 'I'" rule discussed earlier. Here, you're bringing yourself into the picture even before mentioning your company name.) It immediately establishes the problem faced by the reader and builds trust. The next step, of course, is to present the solution in the form of your products or services.

AVOID FLAT LANGUAGE

There is no more boring sentence than one that begins with *There is, There are,* or *It is.* (I just did it there—did you notice how boring it was?) These devices tend to put unnecessary distance between you and the reader.

In fairness, starting one or two sentences with "It is . . ." won't kill your message. (A good thing, too, because I'm certainly guilty of that throughout this book.) But try to be flexible, and look for opportunities to add a more dynamic element to your language.

Instead of

> There are a number of reasons why you should try Acme Widgets, beginning with . . .

try

> Why should you try Acme Widgets? For a number of reasons, beginning with . . .

The altered sentence is punchier—proving once again that you can throw one or two sentence fragments into the mix. Also, note the use of the rhetorical question.

Instead of

> It is becoming more and more common for companies like yours to outsource their back-office operations.

try

> For more and more companies like yours, outsourcing back-office
> operations is a common practice.

Here, the altered sentence puts the client's perspective ("companies like
yours") up front.

PERSONALIZE IT

If you're sending out a one-on-one letter or e-mail, especially if it's a follow-up
note, use your client's name in the body of the letter *once*. Place it near the close
of the letter, ideally in the call to action. It personalizes the message and breaks
down a bit of the implied wall between you and your prospect.

However, if you do it more than once in a letter, you run the risk of coming
across like a suspiciously overeager used-car salesperson.

Avoid

> Let me tell you, Dave, this deal is the best one out there. And Dave, I
> think you'll agree that your company would benefit from real savings. So
> thanks for reading, Dave!

Try

> As I mentioned last week, Dave, I am available to present my company's
> services in person, at your convenience. Please let me know a time that
> works for you.

or

> Please take a look at our Web site, XYZCorp-US.com, for more details on our services. Thanks for your time, Dave. I will follow up with you in the next couple of weeks to discuss how XYZ can help with your inventory management needs.

SOFTEN THE NEGATIVE

When a prospect offers unpleasant feedback or specific objections to your product or service, your natural instinct might be either to get defensive about it or to try to change the subject. But you're better off responding in a more thoughtful, effective way.

I don't need to tell you rule 1 of sales messaging, but I'll say it anyway: *Don't lie*. If the buyer brings up some less-than-flattering bit of information and you respond with a false assurance or blatant exaggeration, you're in deep because now it's in writing.

So let's assume that the prospect has brought up something that you have determined to be certifiably untrue. Politely but firmly correct the record using connective terms such as *however* or *in fact*.

> I appreciate your concerns about Acme's imported goods. However, you have my complete assurance that our products meet all existing regulatory standards. I have attached our official compliance statement.

or

> Thanks for your feedback. I want to emphasize that when factoring in the significant value of our bonus merchandising programs, your rate this year will in fact be slightly lower than last year's.

If, on the other hand, the customer has raised a legitimate concern, you can admit the problem by not really admitting it. Don't start with a flat-out *mea culpa* followed by a *but* statement—it sounds shaky and reduces your leverage in negotiation. Instead, start by using words such as *don't* or *can't* in your admission, and then quickly flip it to a positive statement.

Instead of

> True, XYZ Corp. has had some management changes recently, but we are committed to long-term stability.

try (italics added for illustrative purposes):

> While *we don't* deny that XYZ Corp. has had some management changes recently, we are committed to long-term stability.

Instead of

> While it's true that XYZ Corp. was hit by the mortgage crisis, we have weathered the storm and continue to provide industry-leading loans.

try

> While *it can't be said* that XYZ Corp. was immune to the mortgage crisis, we have weathered the storm and continue to provide industry-leading loans.

In these examples, the reader may mentally skip over the terms *we don't* and *it can't be said*, instead focusing on the more positive aspects of the message.

Finally, keep in mind that if you're going to challenge a specific assertion made by the prospect, you'd better have verifiable information behind it.

PLAY IT UP

The ellipsis (. . .) and the em dash (—) are devices that allow you to emphasize an important phrase. Use them if you're trying to draw more attention to a particular point or if you want to add drama to the message. You don't always want to give away your payoff early in the sentence.

Instead of

> XYZ Corp.'s Exedium line of widgets is the most respected name in the industry.

try

> XYZ Corp. produces the Exedium line of widgets—the most respected name in the industry.

By breaking up the flow of a simple sentence with an em dash, you snap the reader to attention.

Instead of

> Acme Corp. is dedicated to your core customers, who are avid photographers.

try

> Acme Corp. is dedicated to avid photographers—your core customers.

Notice how the payoff ("your core customers") has been shifted to the end of the sentence, after the em dash, thus boosting the impact.

An ellipsis also can be used to add a bit of drama or anticipation, but its more traditional use is to condense a long quotation.

> The widget industry has long been waiting for a database solution that reduces costs and increases efficiency . . . two critical goals achieved by WidgetData 3000.

The colon (:) can be used this way as well (see "Grammar Usage and Form" in Chapter 6 for more details).

One formatting note: When using most word-processing programs, an em dash is created automatically when you type a word, then two hyphens in a row, and then another word, all with no spaces between. In an e-mail, indicate an em dash by typing either two hyphens (--) or a single hyphen separated on either side by a space (-).

PLAY IT DOWN

Parentheses traditionally are used to set off a piece of information or an explanation that isn't entirely critical to the main point. In terms of your sales message, they can be used to soften a necessary but unflattering bit of news or information that you'd like to downplay. Anything you put inside parentheses will be given less emphasis by the reader—think of this device as a kind of "express train" in which the scenery blurs past until the reader gets to the next stop.

For example, let's say that your client has some concerns about your company's financial performance. You can explain it in parentheses as part of an effort to soften the overall impact.

> While there's no disputing that Acme Corp. posted a recent loss (the result of a third-quarter restructuring), the company's long-term financial future is secure.

Or let's say that you've had a product recall.

> While we can't deny that XYZ has faced the occasional challenge with overseas suppliers, this particular issue (the result of a manufacturing decision by a third-party subcontractor) has been resolved quickly and responsibly by our production team.

Now let's say that you're communicating an offer, and you need to include a disclaimer or hedge. You could relegate the disclaimer to a footnote in tiny type at the bottom of the page, but that usually necessitates adding a telltale asterisk. If you're writing an e-mail, it's even tougher to hide disclaimer text. Parentheses, on the other hand, allow you to downplay any qualifying statements even as you present the offer.

> XYZ offers plans as low as $24.95 a month (depending on your local area).

> Sign up by March 31, and you'll receive 0% financing (certain restrictions apply).

As with all devices, use parentheses sparingly. On the stylistic front, put your punctuation inside the closing parenthesis if the phrase is a self-contained sentence and follows a completed sentence; otherwise, put the punctuation outside the closing parenthesis.

KEEP IT REAL

Your clients or prospects can spot phony, clichéd statements a mile away. Instead of making hackneyed claims, give your message the *perception* of truth. This counts particularly for any claim you make regarding measurements of time.

For example, your prospect probably has heard this more than once:

I need just five minutes of your time to explain Acme Corp.'s . . .

But she probably hasn't heard

By giving me just six minutes of your time, you'll see Acme Corp.'s . . .

Your prospect probably has heard this:

Our new townhouses are just a quick, 15-minute drive to downtown.

But he probably hasn't heard

The average drive to downtown from our new townhouses is just 16 minutes.

Your prospect probably has heard the cliché

> I promise to work around the clock to make sure that you're satisfied with our service.

But has he heard the weight of truth:

> workdays between 8:00 a.m. and 7:00 p.m., you can call me if you have any questions or comments about our service. If you reach my voice mail during off-hours, I will respond as quickly as possible.

In each of these examples, the second sentence sounds more real, as though you've put some actual thought into it. Just be able to deliver, of course. If you claim that your real estate properties are a 16-minute commute to downtown, you'd better have tested it by timing your own drive.

EXPAND OR COMPRESS TIME

Here's another way to play with units of time. In general, the way people react to numbers depends on which unit of measurement is used. Put in other terms, the word that immediately follows a number actually determines a person's reaction to the information more than does the number itself.

If you're trying to emphasize speed of service or delivery, consider that

- "60 minutes" appears to be less time than "one hour" because *minute* is a smaller unit than *hour*.
- "30 days" appears to be less than "one month."
- "We can turn it around in 24 hours" appears to be less time than "We can turn it around in one day."

Conversely, if your company is offering a certain service for an impressive length of time, use the larger term of measurement.

- "We'll give you one full month free" appears to be a better deal than "We'll give you 30 days free."
- "The batteries have enough power for two full days of operation" sounds better than "The batteries have enough power for 48 hours of operation."

(Note the addition of the word *full* here—it brings even more heft to the claim.)

This rule about expanding or compressing time really works only when the measurements are presented conversationally. If you're showcasing units of time (or any other measurement) in research tables or charts, you should adhere to the generally accepted numeric guidelines established by your field or industry.

PLAY THE PERCENTAGES

You can make a percentage figure seem more impressive, particularly when it comes to describing market penetration, by not actually mentioning the percentage at all. For example, let's say that your company services 16 percent of all commercial mortgage loans in the local area. To the average person, that figure may not seem very high. However, if you reframe the point, it adds impact.

> Acme Mortgage Co. services nearly 1 of every 6 commercial mortgages in the local area.

Again, while 16 percent may not sound like a lot, "nearly 1 of every 6" does. This is so despite the fact that both figures describe basically the same thing. (The word *every* is optional here—it adds a little punch.) It should be used only when the numeral 1 is the first part of the ratio ("1 of every 5," "1 of every 8," etc.). Also note that "1 in . . ." can be substituted for "1 of. . . ."

On this subject, always bring the ratio down to the lowest common denominator because lower numbers are easier to digest. If, for instance, 1,000 widget companies exist, and you serve 311 of them, don't say, "We reach more than 30 out of 100." Instead, say, "We reach more than 3 in 10."

A quick note about usage: Elsewhere in this book I state that numbers lower than 10 should be written in full (*one, two,* etc.). The tip about percentages, discussed above, is an exception: From a visual standpoint, "1 in 10" has more impact than "one in 10."

TIE THE FUTURE TO THE PRESENT

If you're trying to get your prospect to respond to a limited-time offer, you can make the offer sound more urgent by connecting something in the future to the present.

Instead of

> This offer will expire in 30 days.

try

This offer will expire 30 days from now.

Instead of

Your taxes are due in just six weeks. Do you have the right accountant?

try

Just six weeks from now, your taxes will be due. Do you have the right accountant?

Instead of

In two weeks, new regulations will take effect, marking a profound change in our industry.

try

> Two weeks from today, new regulations will take effect, marking a profound change in our industry.

GIVE THEM A DEADLINE

On a similar note, one of the tried-and-true stratagems of direct marketing is the deadline pitch: "Hurry! This offer is only good until April 30!" Most of the time, this pressure is about as real as a late-night infomercial that urges you to "Call in the next 15 minutes and we'll throw in a second pet grooming tool, free!" However, the deadline has a place in sales letters—as long as it's used in context.

If your letter is of a time-sensitive nature—or you just want to make it seem that way—mention a deadline that has significance to your target audience, and then give your reader the incentive to respond right away.

> The holidays will be here shortly, and that means it's time to think about sourcing gifts for all your clients. If you get back to me by November 15, you'll be locked in to our preferred rate on a wide range of corporate gifts.

> As you know, new postal regulations take effect on August 1 of this year. Is your company prepared? Call or e-mail me by June 30, and you'll qualify for preincrease printing rates.

I see that next June officially marks your company's 50th anniversary—congratulations. If you're considering a milestone event to commemorate the occasion, the time is now to start planning. We can help. Contact me in the next 14 days, and I'll ensure that you are locked in to this year's rates.

CHANGE HISTORY

Let's say that you're trying to play up your company's long and impressive history. Stating the number of years you've been in business is more powerful than just mentioning your founding year. Also, keep in mind the rules about expanding or compressing time: The larger the unit of measurement, the longer it seems like you've been around.

Instead of

Our company has been serving the community since 1938.

try

Our company has been serving the community for more than 70 years.

Even better:

> Our company has been serving the community for over seven decades.

A couple of caveats about this one: First, if you're going to assign approximate numbers to anything ("more than 40 years," "nearly 100 employees," etc.), make sure that the number itself is rounded. I've always chuckled a bit whenever I've seen sales literature that includes something like, "We've been in business for over 37 years." What does that mean? That you've been in business for 37 years and 3 months? Or, "We've won more than 23 industry awards." Um, does that mean you've won 24 awards? In these cases, it's better to say, "nearly 40 years" and "more than 20 industry awards," respectively.

Second, by saying that you've been in business for a specific number of years, you automatically date the message. If it's a standard letter or e-mail, no problem (just keep updating the message as time moves on). If you're doing a printed, glossy piece that you expect to keep in the field for a couple of years, though, you might want to revert to using the date of your company's founding, because that will never change.

TURN THE TABLES ON THE COMPETITION

If you're trying to pry a client away from a competitor, it's sometimes better to focus on what the prospect would *not* get if he or she decides to go with that competitor.

Instead of

> XYZ Corp. offers you more for your money. By signing up with us, you'll get 20% more widgets compared with a similarly priced plan from our nearest competitor.

try

XYZ Corp. offers you more for your money. Customers of our nearest competitor, on the other hand, get 20% *fewer* widgets from a similarly priced plan.

Instead of

With XYZ Auto Insurance, you'll pay an average of $500 a year less than customers of the largest carrier.

try

Compared with XYZ Auto Insurance policyholders, customers of the largest carrier pay an average of $500 *more* per year.

AVOID NAMING NAMES

On a related note, you're better off referring to your competitors anonymously instead of by name—it lets you take the high road, and it avoids giving your competition more name recognition. Besides, if you do it right, your reader will have a pretty good idea of the organization to which you are referring.

When making a comparison with competitors, don't just refer to them by using a blanket generality ("other providers," "other companies in the field," etc.). This is too vague and doesn't give the reader any real frame of reference.

Instead, define the competition on your terms. For example, if you're the new kid in an established field, you can slyly nod to your larger rivals by tagging them with less-than-desirable traits while at the same time elevating yourself into their league.

> Our corporate competitors . . .
> Our larger, less-flexible competition . . .
> Our less-tech-savvy competition . . .

Conversely, if you're the leader who's trying to bat away the upstarts, you can raise questions about these rivals with such terms as

> The newer, less-experienced players . . .
> The recent entrants into the field . . .
> The smaller companies with fewer resources . . .

Whatever you do, avoid calling any single competitor *the leading provider* or *the industry leader*. This is a subjective statement, and you don't want to be the one making it. Use a more quantitative descriptor such as *the largest provider* or *the original provider in the field*. If you happen to be number one in your field in some quantitative measure, refer to the number two company as your *nearest competitor*.

If the competition's name must come up in your correspondence, limit it to notes that come later in the sales process, that is, if you're addressing specific objections or questions.

TELL THEM YOU'RE THE ONE

Similarly, to set yourself apart from the competition without mentioning your rivals' names, let your clients know that you represent the *one* company that meets their needs. As an adjective, the word *one*—or the combination *only one*—is extremely powerful and has more impact than *only* ("We're the only company to . . .") or *sole* ("We're the sole company to . . .").

To keep the drama at maximum strength, construct your statement so that your company or product is the last thing mentioned in the sentence, following a colon or an em dash.

> Claims of eco-friendly practices are made almost daily in the widget business. But only one company has made a full commitment to sustainable business practices across its spectrum of operations: Acme Corp.

> Amid the questionable lending practices of the past several years, one bank has maintained its exceptionally high standards for the security and well-being of its customers—XYZ Trust.

A variation is to channel *The Matrix* and describe yourself or your company as *the one*.

> As the one licensed real estate agent in our region to win the coveted XYZ Service Award, I will bring an unmatched level of professionalism and care to our working relationship.

As always, whenever you're throwing down the gauntlet like this, you'd better be able to back up your claim.

BE CONFIDENT

Want to seal the deal? Write as if you've already done so. In the direct-marketing business, this is called an *assumed close*. It means that you're communicating with your prospect as though he or she is already a confirmed client, and you're getting ready to start the partnership.

On the surface, this technique might seem a little presumptuous—and maybe a little arrogant—but if it is done subtly enough, it can move the prospect's decision-making needle just a little closer in your direction. It's especially effective as part of the call to action in the closing paragraph of the letter.

> I'm looking forward to putting together a plan that meets YourBrand's needs for the coming fiscal year and beyond.

> When you choose to partner with Acme Corp., you've made an outstanding strategic decision that will pay off in maximized productivity, savings, and revenue opportunities.

> I will contact you shortly to begin discussing ideas for the growth of your business.

UNDERPROMISE, OVERDELIVER

Surely you've heard this in your sales training: Keep your claims fairly modest, and then wow the client with your ability to go beyond expectations. You've done it time and again in your face-to-face pitches, but how do you do it in writing?

It's especially important to temper your claims in a letter or e-mail because it's hard to scale back an unrealistic expectation once you drop the letter in the mail or click on "Send." Fortunately, you've got some very simple linguistic devices at your disposal for the purpose of hedging your bets. The simplest solution? Substitute *can* for *will* ("We *can* help you achieve . . ." instead of "We *will* help you achieve . . ."). Or add the phrase *up to* or *as many as* when making quantitative claims.

Some examples (italics added here for emphasis):

> Acme Corp. *can help* YourBrand generate impressive gains in customer satisfaction.

> Our clients have experienced *up to* a 40% increase in operational efficiency.

XYZ Corp.'s WowSoft technology is *designed to improve* server performance.

Acme Financial *can put you on the road* to a secure retirement.

Recently, my clients have received *as many as* five offers on their homes within 36 hours.

XYZ Corp. *can put your company in a position to* achieve substantial revenue growth.

Signing up with us is *the first step toward* significant savings in your monthly telecommunications expenses.

> Acme Corp.'s Excellentus is a smart solution for companies *committed to* cutting costs in their back-office operations.

DON'T JUST DECIDE; MAKE A DECISION

In Chapter 6 you'll find a tip that encourages you to use economical language—saying something in two or three words instead of five or six. Here's an exception where using three or four words is better than using one.

You can add impact by substituting a simple declarative verb for a construction of the word *made* (e.g., *decided* versus *made the decision*). It sounds as if you've put a considerable amount of time, thought, or energy into the statement that follows. It also sounds firmer and, well, more decisive.

Instead of

> We could have skimped on quality, but we chose to invest in strong design.

try (italics added here for emphasis)

> We could have skimped on quality, but we *made the choice* to invest in strong design.

Instead of

> Based on my discussion with management, we decided to reduce your rate by 10%.

try

> Based on my discussion with management, we have *made a decision* to reduce your rate by 10%.

Let's say that after much back and forth, you're delivering a final offer. Instead of

> Having attempted to accommodate each of your requests, we can offer the following . . .

try

> Having *made every effort* to accommodate each of your requests, we are prepared to offer the following . . .

As an alternative, you can use *came to the conclusion* to indicate decisiveness or deliberation (e.g., "We came to the conclusion that . . ." versus "We decided that . . .").

MAKE THEM FEEL SPECIAL

Everyone wants preferential treatment—that special deal or arrangement that the other person down the street *isn't* getting. In your sales letters, give the perception that the reader is being let in on privileged information or an uncommon deal. Such words as *exclusive, preferred, rare, private,* and *privileged* can serve this purpose. As always, though, heed the rule of moderation.

> You have an exclusive opportunity to experience a level of business travel that was once available only to the world's most powerful CEOs.

> As a key decision maker within the widget industry, you are entitled to a private consultation and preferential rate package with XYZ Corp.

> You'll get a privileged suite of software and services normally reserved only for our largest corporate clients.

One exception: Avoid the word *unique*. It may well be the most overrated term in sales communications—used so often that it has lost all meaning. Unless you're selling items that are truly one of a kind (e.g., diamonds, hand-made art, etc.), it's best to pitch your product or service as something like *distinctive, singular,* or *inimitable,* which gives you a little more poetic license. And don't make an empty claim—you'd better be able to prove just how different you are.

LET THEM KNOW THE WAIT IS OVER

As discussed earlier in this book, the first two building blocks of a good sales letter are (1) establishing a problem or challenge faced by your prospect and (2) presenting your product or service as the solution to the issue. A good way to lead into the solution is to use language that emphasizes a feeling of relief or delivers an "Aha!" moment. Terms such as *finally* and *at last* drive home the point that your client's long search for answers is over.

> Finally, you've found an outsourced hiring solution built to fit your company's changing needs.

> Smart investors like you have long been searching for a trustworthy resource to help generate reliable retirement income. At last, an answer is at hand: Acme Corp. Financial Services.

LET YOUR CUSTOMERS SELL FOR YOU

If you've got a particularly strong testimonial quote from a valued customer, use it. In this age of consumer empowerment and user-generated content, you can benefit greatly from having your current clients spread the word to prospective clients.

In terms of placement, add the endorsement to a supporting paragraph. It lends substance to a sales claim.

> By making the switch to Acme Insurance, you can save not just money but also time. Susan Jones of Anytown, TX, is one of the thousands of Acme customers who can attest to this: "I saved $500 a year over my previous carrier," says Susan, "and my claim was handled much quicker."

If the quote is a ringing endorsement from a well-known individual or company, don't bury it. Billboard it above the letter's salutation, or showcase it as its own paragraph somewhere in the letter. If the quote is concise enough, you can even indent it and highlight it in boldface type.

> **"Acme Corp.'s Dynamo 5000 software has been the single biggest factor in our productivity growth."**
> —*Sally Q. Mediastar, FamousCorp*

You'll occasionally need to sharpen your editing skills when dealing with testimonials. Take a good look at that endorsement from your customer. It might go something like this:

Thank you so much! Everyone here at the home office of XYZ Manufacturing was absolutely thrilled with the service we got from Bill and his team at Acme Corp. They were really responsive and met all of our needs in a timely, cost-effective manner. We will definitely work together again, and we're all looking forward to it. We just can't say enough great things about what a wonderful job Bill did!

If you were to run this verbatim, you'd be sacrificing valuable space that could be used for other key sales points. Buried amid all the gushing in this quote is the heart of the endorsement; it's up to you to dig it out. And yes, you have the right to pare down a direct quote to its core, as long as you don't change the fundamental meaning. Here's how the preceding quote might look in edited form:

"XYZ Manufacturing is thrilled with the service we got from the team at Acme Corp. They were really responsive and met all of our needs in a timely, cost-effective manner. We will definitely work together again."

Now go back and compare the two. You'll see that the meaning is still there in the edited version. (The word *was* has been changed to *is* in the first sentence of the revised quote, but it doesn't affect the meaning.) The details about timeliness and cost-effectiveness are still there. The kicker ("We will definitely work together again") is still there.

When it comes to sourcing the quote, the more specific you are, the better. It lends more credibility to the statement. Instead of

> One of our top manufacturing clients says, "Acme Corp. is the best. . . ."

try

> Joe Smith, purchasing director of XYZ Manufacturing, says, "Acme Corp. is the best. . . ."

Of, course, only use the customer's full name, job title, and/or company name with his or her permission (and make sure that the client has cleared it with his or her own management). If you don't get permission, you're within your rights to run the quote anonymously—it's better than no quote at all. (Just make sure that the anonymous testimonial doesn't reveal key identifying details about the person or the company.)

One more time: *Heed the rule of moderation.* A couple of testimonials are more than enough for one letter.

MAKE A CASE OUT OF IT

Want to go a step beyond the client endorsement? Bring in the client case study. This is an extended description, in your own words, of how you've helped a key client overcome specific hurdles and achieve business growth. It's a good alternative to the standard opening paragraph, helping you to establish the challenge, the solution, and, ideally, your core idea.

Avoid the temptation to ramble. Your mission: Tell a compelling, persuasive story—one that ends with a clear, memorable sales point—in a single paragraph.

Anything longer than this and you've squandered a good chunk of your valuable space.

If you have clearance to mention the client's name in the case study, feel free to use it as you would with a direct testimonial. (Seeing that a competitor is using your services might be just the motivation a prospect needs to jump on the bandwagon.)

My preference, however, is to keep it anonymous. It adds intrigue, allowing your prospects to see a little of themselves in the story. And while direct client quotes are often generic statements of praise, case studies represent a good opportunity to show off specific statistics about business growth or performance. Most of your clients will not want this information revealed publicly, so your best bet is to keep the name under wraps.

> Not long ago, the engineers at an industrial manufacturer like yours determined that increased costs and competition required the company to produce its powertrains faster and more cost-effectively and to make its enterprise IT infrastructure more efficient. Who did they turn to? XYZ Corp. and our Wow5000 processor platform. The result: significant, energy-efficient performance gains, as well as a 30% reduction in computational time and a 15% decrease in total cost of ownership—all of which positions the company for further growth.

> Recently, a business owner like you left his enterprise in trust, with the intention of selling it for the benefit of his daughter. To help navigate the sale, he appointed a trustee with longtime expertise in family business. The trustee obtained a favorable valuation of the business, resolved issues with existing company management, and achieved higher

continued on next page

> proceeds by separating the sale of the company's real estate from the sale of its equipment and other assets. This successful exit strategy translated to more than $5 million for the beneficiary. The experts who engineered it? Acme Trust.

> Last year, a regional supermarket chain—a midsize firm like yours—was seeking to standardize its staff scheduling and forecasting across multiple stores in several states. The company turned to a breakthrough Web-based workforce optimization system. Within a year of its implementation, sales had improved by an average of 4% across its locations, and administrative time had been reduced by 45%. Most important, the company had created a consistent, standardized experience for management, employees, and customers alike—all with the help of XYZ Workforce Solutions.

In all these examples, you can see that a conscious attempt has been made to tie the circumstances and fortunes of the anonymous client to those of the prospect. The prospect's ideal reaction should be: "Hey, my peers and competitors are making gains by going with this provider. Why shouldn't I give it a shot?"

Because you have so much detail to impart in a case study, sometimes you aren't able to get to a full expression of the core idea. No problem—this is one of those cases in which it's okay to put off the core idea until the second paragraph. You can hit the core idea by immediately following the case study with a transitional statement that directly addresses the prospect. In the first example on page 82, the next paragraph might begin

> The opportunity for this kind of business transformation is now available to your firm. The Wow5000 processor platform from XYZ Corp. is a smart, proven solution for the IT and engineering challenges you face every day.

Now you've gotten all the big stuff out of the way: challenge, solution, and core idea. You can then begin outlining your supporting points.

MAKE THEM SMILE

You might have been combing through this book and noticed that few, if any, of the writing examples feature quips or other funny stuff. You might be saying to yourself, "I'm a fun-loving person with a great sense of humor, and my customers adore me because I'm always quick with the jokes. What about bringing in my own personality? Why can't I throw in a few one-liners here and there to loosen things up?"

The short answer is, you most definitely can. However—and I apologize for being the downer at the party—certain restrictions apply. Bear in mind that what's sidesplitting to you may be only mildly amusing or even offensive to your prospect. (To quote from the film *This Is Spinal Tap*, "There's a fine line between clever and stupid.") So tread with caution.

Force-fitting a joke into your letter merely for the sake of injecting your personality isn't the way to go. Humor works best when it's a natural fit within the context of your message *and* it makes a sales point.

A bit of humor, for example, can entice a prospect to keep reading up to your core idea.

Some statistics don't reveal much. As David Letterman once said, "*USA Today* has come out with a new survey. Apparently, three out of four people make up 75% of the population." But one new statistic reveals a great deal about the widget industry: 60% of CEOs say that they will outsource critical functions this year. When you need expert, reliable outsourcing services, turn to XYZ Inc.—the solution for a growing number of companies.

Speaking of people like Letterman, using the name of a famous personality is a good way to grab attention. Just make sure that the quoted person has some relevance to your audience (keep in mind their demographics) and isn't too controversial.

Sometimes the answers to the biggest business challenges are the simplest. Steve Martin once said, "I've got to keep breathing. It'll be my worst business mistake if I don't." While the key to expanding into international markets might not be quite that elementary, it's just become a little clearer. For 25 years, Acme Consulting has helped clients across a number of industry sectors to plan and execute their international business strategies successfully.

If you're going to tell a humorous story with a classic setup, make sure that you lead into it with some kind of statement that foreshadows the solution to follow.

> What's the difference between success and failure in sales? The answer may lie in an old joke: Years ago, an American shoe company sent two sales reps to different parts of the Australian outback to see if they could sell their products to the Aborigines. Later, the first rep sent a message to the home office: "Forget it. Natives don't wear shoes." Separately, the second rep said, "Great opportunity. Natives don't wear shoes!" We at Acme Corp. know you're in the latter camp. So we want to give you every chance to succeed . . . with our proven lead-management software.

To sum up: Use humor to pique their interest, but don't let it overwhelm or detract from your basic sales message.

GIVE THEM A GIFT

So far, this book has dealt exclusively with the substance of your letters, not sales gimmicks or incentives. But one incentive is worth addressing: the use of small gifts or premiums attached to your letter.

If you're pitching a very small number of high-value clients—or maybe just one prized prospect—and you want to make a splash, an unusual or attention-getting item sent with the letter is a good way to do it. (This rule, of course, applies only to mailed cover letters—with e-mails, you don't have this luxury.)

It doesn't need to be expensive—in fact, it shouldn't be, because many companies have stringent rules about the maximum value of gifts from salespeople. Just make it something that is physically compact and ideally has some utility for the recipient. If it's going to several people, make sure that it's unisex (usable for men and women); if it's going to men only or women only, you can get more gender-targeted.

It doesn't even need to have any real connection to your company's products or services. Just be able, in your cover note, to come up with a metaphor that makes a relevant, memorable point linking the *benefit* of the item to the *benefit* of your services.

A few thought starters:

Gift item: Mini-picture frame
Sample cover note:
Please keep the enclosed frame for your favorite snapshot. At the same time, take a mental snapshot of your business at this very moment: Is it achieving maximum productivity? Picture a brighter future for your organization—with support from XYZ Consultants.

Gift item: Packets of tea
Sample cover note:
One simple fact about tea is that the longer it brews, the stronger the result it achieves. A similar truth applies to Acme Corp.: We've been brewing up software solutions for the widget industry for 20 years, and the results we deliver are more robust than ever.

Gift item: Mini-flashlight
Sample cover note:
You know who your main customers are. But have you looked in every last corner for new prospects? Like the enclosed flashlight—yours to keep, with our compliments—the database from XYZ Corp. can help you to effectively spotlight the names you may be missing.

Avoid clichéd items such as pens or coffee mugs. And keep in mind what your recipients do for a living. If, for example, they work for a wine company, don't send a wine opener; if they work for a computer company, don't send a flash drive. They've probably got several of those already.

Chapter 4

The Art of Text and E-Mail

Right there in large type on the cover of this book is the phrase *Winning Sales Letters*. When you hear the word *letter*, what image do you get? Is it someone wearing a fedora and smoking a stogie while pecking away on an old manual typewriter? Someone in a powdered wig scribbling with a quill pen? No surprise. Among business professionals, the term has become somewhat dated, as in, "No one writes letters anymore, do they?" The truth, however, is that any business correspondence to an outside party—whether by e-mail, text message, or hand-written thank-you note—is a letter.

E-mail is firmly ensconced as the prevailing method of written business communication throughout the world. The beauty of it is that it's a lot cheaper and more eco-conscious than printed communications, and you can get a much quicker response if a prospect is interested in your message. In addition, the vast majority of business-to-business and business-to-consumer audiences have come to expect sales pitches delivered electronically. As I mentioned earlier, it's likely that apart from the introductory note, most of your ongoing correspondence with prospects and clients will be by e-mail (assuming, of course, that you have access to their e-mail addresses).

Just because e-mails are quicker and easier to create and send than printed letters, however doesn't mean that you should ignore this book's general rules when communicating electronically.

Take a good look at the e-mails you've received from friends and colleagues. Chances are that a fair number of them are hastily and sloppily written. For some reason, the instant, spontaneous nature of e-mail causes a lot of people to cast aside any regard for style, form, or accuracy—all in the name of firing off that quick note *now*.

Even more of a free-for-all is short message service (SMS), otherwise known as *text messaging*. Unfolding like a frantically typed transcript of a real-time conversation, *texting* is a paradox. While it's among the most technologically advanced forms of personal communication, it is also, with its coded abbreviations and general lack of discipline, among the most primitive and chaotic.

Needless to say, you should be as clear and professional in your e-mails—and even your text messages—as you are in your printed letters. Your client probably has just deleted dozens of junk e-mails and unsolicited pitches before he or she opens your note. With just a few precious seconds in which to grab that person's attention, your message had better be compelling, well written, and to the point.

FOLLOW THE RULES

First, if you're a U.S.-based entity sending a mass e-mail to a large prospect database, make sure that you're in compliance with the CAN-SPAM Act. Signed into U.S. law in 2003, CAN-SPAM offers consumers protection against unwanted e-mails. Here's a brief overview of what you need to do to stay within the letter of the law:

- Your "From" information must accurately identify you as the sender of the e-mail, including your full domain name and e-mail address.
- Your subject line cannot mislead the prospect about the contents or subject matter of the message.
- You must include an opt-out method: a return e-mail address or Web link that allows a recipient to request that you not send future messages to that e-mail address. You must honor any such request within 10 days of receiving it.
- Your message must contain clear and conspicuous language stating that the message is a solicitation and that the recipient can opt out of receiving further commercial e-mail from you. It also must include your valid postal address.

KNOW YOUR AUDIENCE

As wonderful as e-mail is, it's not always your default mode of communication with prospects. If you're pitching directly to consumers and you have a database of e-mail addresses, it doesn't necessarily mean that e-mail is the best way to reach these prospects. Do the research. If these individuals—whether owing to minimal computer access, knowledge, or interest—seem less likely to use e-mail on a regular basis, start off by sending them a printed letter. Include your e-mail address in the call to action. If they respond via e-mail instead of by phone, now you've got your opening to continue the discussion electronically.

Or if you're promoting a product or service that is very high-end or creative and demands a certain level of aesthetic presentation, you're probably better off introducing yourself through a thoughtful, well-crafted letter in a tastefully designed envelope. In this case, even if you've initiated contact via printed letter, you still can switch to e-mail for all follow-up and strategic communications throughout the sales process.

Conversely, if your target audience is tech-savvy "twentysomethings" accustomed to planning their entire lives online, stay away from the printed letter and use e-mail from the start. Younger consumers not only are wary of anything that comes via "snail mail," but they're also even a bit put off by the idea of face-to-face business interactions. As author and columnist Penelope Trunk writes in her "Brazen Careerist" blog, "Often, an in-person sales pitch to a young person is like an IM message blinking on-screen to a baby boomer: unwanted interruption of information processing."

BREAK IT UP

The major difference between e-mails and printed letters is that with an e-mail, you have less space in which to make your point. Just as no one wants to read a rambling, three-page letter, no one has time to read an e-mail that scrolls for two full screens.

Use the brevity and spontaneity of e-mail to your advantage. Let's say that you have a series of points to make, building to a big finale or special offer. Don't try to cram all your pitch into a single message—the recipient will open it to reveal a sea of text and most likely reach for the "Delete" button. Instead, parcel out the various points over the course of a few days as a kind of "teaser" campaign.

On Monday, send a quick e-mail pertaining to your core idea and a single supporting point; a few days later, send supporting point 2; and a few days after that, send supporting point 3 along with a persuasive offer.

Example sent on Monday:

Subject: Ditch the airlines: Reason number 1 from Acme

Dear Jeff:

As the owner of a midsize business, you're all too familiar with the hassles of commercial air travel: inevitable delays, cramped seats, ever-increasing business-class fares. In our region, plenty of entrepreneurs like you have been able to ditch the airlines and fly privately, thanks to Acme Aviation. We're one of the most experienced aviation sales and leasing firms in the Southeast, with the most flexible buying programs for a wide range of customers.

Here's the first reason why it makes sense to ditch the airlines: Acme Aviation actually makes private jet ownership affordable. Our innovative FlyRite financing plans will put you into the exact aircraft you want, within your specific budget.

Example sent on Thursday (three business days later):

Subject: Ditch the airlines: Reason number 2 from Acme

Dear Jeff:

The other day, I contacted you to tell you about the financial benefits of ditching the airlines through a flexible private jet financing program with Acme Aviation. Today, I want to address another crucial factor: flexibility. I'm sure you've never heard that word from the airlines, with their inconvenient flight schedules and bare-bones amenities.

You will hear it when you work with Acme, however. You'll find a wide range of proven aircraft to fit the needs of your business, from the latest high-tech light jets to painstakingly restored preowned models.

Example sent the following Tuesday (three business days later):

Subject: Ditch the airlines: Free services from Acme

Dear Jeff:

You've heard me tell you about how flexible and affordable it is to fly privately with Acme Aviation. Well, I have one last reason why it pays for you to ditch the airlines, and it's the biggest one: customer service. (Try, for example, getting help at the airline counter!)

With Acme, your aircraft purchase is just the beginning. We're with you throughout the entire ownership experience, with outstanding service options, such as our Wings Plan, and a dedicated customer contact.

If you're willing to invest a few minutes in a phone conversation with me, I'll not only get you into an Acme FlyRite leasing program, but I'll also start you with one free year of our Wings Plan.

Make sure that in each message you include a clear call to action and multiple options for contact. Also notice that messages two and three start with references to the point made in the previous e-mail—this is done to refresh the prospect's memory or to hedge in case he or she didn't read the earlier message.

In the first two messages, include brief language letting the prospect know that there's more to follow—giving a heads-up to expect another message in a few days.

Here is an example of a call to action for messages one or two:

Thanks for reading, Jeff. A few days from now, you'll get the next piece of the puzzle regarding the benefits of ditching the airlines. In the meantime,

continued on next page

---

please visit AcmeAviationSales.com for the full story. If you have any questions, feel free to contact me at myname@AcmeAviation Sales.com or 123-456-7890.

OFFER A COMPELLING SUBJECT (LINE)

Back in the horse-and-buggy era—pre-Internet—if you wanted to catch the attention of an important prospect, you'd send a sales letter in an unusual or eye-catching envelope, or you'd send it accompanied by a package with a small gift or interesting premium item. (This latter technique still has the power to persuade; see "Give Them a Gift" in Chapter 3.)

Today, you're more likely to be sending that person an e-mail, and your message makes its appearance among dozens of nearly identical ones stacked up in the recipient's virtual inbox.

You now have only one variable to help you stand out from the pack: your e-mail subject line. In the space of a few carefully chosen words, you have to do what was once accomplished by using a brightly colored envelope or an unusually shaped box.

Here are a few tips for crafting an effective e-mail subject line:

Don't Shout

Avoid the use of all-capital letters, exclamation points, or extraneous random characters. As in Chapter 2, ***IT'S THE EQUIVALENT OF SHOUTING!!!***. The recipient could very well assume that it's spam and delete it without opening it. If you insist on using all-capitals somewhere, keep it to a word or two, preferably your company name.

On a related note, don't become the online equivalent of the Boy Who Cried Wolf. *Never* mark an e-mail "URGENT" unless you're deep in the negotiation process, there's a clock ticking on a looming deadline, and the future of your business is at stake.

Keep It Short

Most e-mail programs set a limit on the number of characters allowed in subject lines. So try to restrict yours to six or seven words. If you serve up a long-winded statement, you will be cut off, and that looks unprofessional.

Within such a short space, don't try to communicate too much. If it's your first contact with the prospect, reference your company's name (if the company is known within the industry) and/or your client's company name, if possible (i.e., if your list is small enough; see the exception for automated mass e-mails later in this chapter). Most important, include a basic benefit.

Subject: Acme Inc.: Productivity solutions for YourBrand

Subject: Efficient customer-service software for YourBrand

Subject: Supertiva: Breakthrough in seasonal allergy treatment

As in the last example above, you might not be able to fit in the client's name, based on the character-count restrictions. Use your judgment.

Work the Angles

In sales, you look for any angle you can. In many cases, your best one is a personal connection that you have with the prospect. If you're coming to the prospect as a referral from someone else, go with that referral as the subject line. If you have room, try to slip in a benefit reference.

> **Subject:** Software solutions referral from Steve Smith

Or if you don't know the prospect but you do know that the prospect (or his or her company) has just gotten news of some kind—good or bad—reference it in the subject line. As long as it's timely and specific, it will not appear to be spam, and the prospect will be intrigued enough to open it. If you have room, tease the topic of the e-mail.

> **Subject:** Congrats on the Widget Award . . . What's next?

> **Subject:** Tough Q4. Here's an idea to turn it around.

Tease the Message

Another persuasive technique is the teaser subject line, which actually can serve as the first few words of the opening paragraph itself. It's a particularly good approach if you're leading with a case study.

If you go this route, make sure that you include some defining characteristic in the subject line that lets the prospect know that it's not a spam message but a legitimate business communication.

> **Subject:** Your peers in the widget business came to us . . .

The connection here is that the sender knows that the prospect is in the widget industry, which separates the sender from the typical spam hurler. The ellipsis (. . .) at the end is an indication that there's more to the statement, which is an entice-ment to open the e-mail.

The e-mail body begins by completing the statement.

> . . . with what they knew was likely an impossible request. But they also knew that the product-development specialists at XYZ, Inc., are experts when it comes to pulling off the impossible. The client, a major player in the widget field, gave us a complex drawing, and our engineers delivered exactly to their specifications. This kind of service is why XYZ, Inc., is the fastest-growing widget-parts supplier in the country.

Get Specific

Similarly, if you're sending information as a follow-up to an initial phone call or face-to-face meeting, make sure to reference something specific so that the recip-ient doesn't mistake the e-mail for spam.

> **Subject:** Following up on our call from Oct. 14

This is better than

> **Subject:** Following up

because the reference to the date of the call is verifiable.

Get Intuitive

Here's another way you can subtly ingratiate yourself to a client: Use intuitive subject lines. By this, I mean if you're talking about volume discounts, use the subject line, "Acme, Inc.: Volume discounts." (Keep your company's name in there if feasible.) In this way, if the client needs to go back and reference the e-mail, he or she can search for it alphabetically by subject line. This is a small courtesy on your part, but an effective one.

If you're engaged in a long series of back-and-forth e-mails and the topic of conversation keeps mutating (e.g., you've gone from discussing volume discounts to value added), don't allow the subject line to read, "Re: Re: Re: Volume discounts." Change it to reflect the new subject at hand. In this way, if the client has to return to check a specific part of the conversation, he or she doesn't have to open a bunch of messages or search text by a vague key word.

USE THE RIGHT TONE

Keep your e-mails friendly but professional—don't type anything you wouldn't say to a client in a conference room full of people. Before you hit "Send," carefully review and confirm the appropriateness and factuality of the information you're conveying. Remember that the term *e-mail trail* has replaced *paper trail* in the lexicon of business deals gone bad.

Finally, unless you've got a longstanding personal friendship with a client, don't use emoticons (symbols or characters such as smiley faces or winks) to punctuate statements. You're a representative of your company, not a teen posting a message to a friend's Facebook Wall. I have an aversion to any kind of emoticon in business e-mails (regardless of the recipient), but that's my taste. If you want to share an in-joke with a friendly client, feel free to tack on your smiley face—but don't overdo it.

SIMPLIFY THE FORMATTING

When writing an e-mail, don't assume that you have carte blanche to use the same visual devices (namely, boldface or italics) that you do when writing a printed letter. In fact, I would recommend against using type formatting for e-mails under any circumstances. Even if your e-mail program allows you to format text (and most do), there's no guarantee that the e-mail will show up in your recipient's inbox looking exactly as you intended.

There's even a risk that the e-mail will appear riddled with bizarre, extraneous characters (e.g., "#Acme^Corp&"). This is especially true if you've created the note in a word processing program and then cut and pasted it into the body of the e-mail. The recipient will just assume that this was your mistake—which doesn't leave the best impression.

So how do you indicate emphasis in an e-mail? Some people choose to hang asterisks around a word that otherwise would be italicized (e.g., "This time, we're delivering even **more** performance"), whereas others use all capitals. Avoid. Neither one looks very professional.

My advice is simply to accept the fact that e-mail is the "flattest" form of communication—it just isn't very good at conveying emotion or emphasis. As Daniel Goleman, author of *Social Intelligence: The New Science of Human Relationships*, wrote in a 2007 essay in the *New York Times*, "E-mail can be emotionally impoverished when it comes to nonverbal messages that add nuance to our words." Therefore, if you have a sentence in an e-mail that cries out for an italicized word, either leave it alone and assume that your reader will get your point or rewrite it to remove any doubt.

When listing bullet points, use asterisks or hyphens.

* Lower rates than the competition
* Award-winning service
* Money-back guarantee

If you want to highlight a subhead within the body of an e-mail, separate it with blank lines above and below, and give it initial caps (e.g., "Clinically Proven Efficacy").

DON'T GET ATTACHED

When an e-mail from an unknown person shows up in my inbox and I see a little paper clip symbol next to it, here's my first reaction: Virus. Spam. Delete. I'd wager that many of your prospects have the same response.

With that in mind, *never* attach a file of any kind to an e-mail unless you have an established business relationship with the recipient, or the recipient is at least expecting your e-mail.

You're probably itching to send a .pdf sell sheet or a quick PowerPoint presentation to show off your products and services, but now is not the time. Limit that initial e-mail to a sharply focused text-only message. After a follow-up meeting or phone call, you're free to start sending digital attachments—and then only with the buyer's permission. (Also try to limit the size of attachments to less than 1 MB because few things are more annoying at work than waiting while a huge file from an outside party is downloading.)

TURN THE MASS E-MAIL INTO THE PERSONAL

Let's say that you've got a massive prospect list, one so big that time constraints make it impossible to send out personalized e-mails. You have no choice but to send a generic message to your database. This is fine as long as you take at least a few measures to give the *impression* that it's personalized—a lesson learned from direct-mail marketing.

As discussed in Chapter 1, you can use an e-mail distribution program merged with your database of customer e-mail addresses to create a note with some degree of personalization. Use these resources to customize fields within the salutation and body of the message. As with printed letters, try to include the recipient's first name in the body, preferably in the call to action.

Following up on a point I made earlier about using the client's name or company in the subject line, I recommend against doing this with a mass e-mail. It's a quality-control issue: Because of character-count limitations, the name might get cut off, and that's bad. If you're sending out hundreds or thousands of these automated e-mails, it's much more difficult to tell whether your subject line will appear as intended in the recipient's inbox.

On a side note, perhaps the biggest concern of all with mass e-mails is privacy. If you're simultaneously sending the same e-mail content to a large group of people, use your own e-mail address in the "Send To" field—it also serves as a confirmation that the message was sent successfully—and "Blind CC" your entire list. You do *not* want your prospects knowing who else is getting the pitch.

MAKE A SPLASH, THEN FOLLOW UP

You may be an ace marketing designer (or have access to one) who can come up with a brilliant-looking graphic e-mail blast, complete with a general sales pitch, slick images, and links to your company's Web site. By all means, you should take advantage of this for your first point of contact with a prospective client.

You have a couple of options here: Either you can make the message image-driven and text-light, serving as a kind of advertisement or online "home page" for your sales pitch, or you can structure it as a kind of mock newsletter, with your sales points arranged as a series of small "articles" or sound bites. Either way, make sure that this e-mail blast has a call to action including your personal contact information, not just your company's Web URL. The best course of action is to ensure that the prospect simply can hit "Reply" to reach you.

If you're quoting outside research, media reviews, or any other information source to back up your sales claims, you might want to include a link to the original source material, assuming that it's available on the Web. This adds credibility to your claims. Just make sure that the link is accurate and working, the site is reputable, and the full content on the Web page is favorable to your message (i.e., if you've edited a media quote to suit your sales pitch but the full review is less than flattering, don't link to it). Since some people are reluctant to follow blind Web links in e-mails from unknown persons, realize that not everyone will click through.

Also keep in mind the general rule about e-mail marketing: Different prospects work on different operating systems and interfaces, so there's no guarantee how your HTML e-mail is going to show up on their screens (e.g., images might not load fully, text might not flow as intended, and so on). Include a link that allows the recipient to view the message on the Web if it's not displaying properly.

The most important thing to note about this first e-mail is that it's just a teaser—a way to whet your prospect's appetite for your products or services. The tougher part comes next: It's your responsibility to send a follow-up e-mail that's more personalized. For this one, it should be a humble all-text e-mail—no bells or whistles necessary. Now it's just you and the prospect, one on one.

HOLD YOUR FIRE

E-mail is great for its spontaneity, but that can backfire on you. You've probably heard the story about Abraham Lincoln and his practice regarding letters: Whenever he wrote a note in anger, he'd set it aside; if, after two days, he felt the same way, he'd actually send it. While the speed of modern business probably necessitates the concentration of that timeframe to a couple of hours instead of a couple of days, it's still important to heed Lincoln's advice when you communicate by e-mail.

If, for example, you've gotten the runaround from a client, it's very tempting to fire off a curt e-mail or text message in frustration. Instead, save it as a draft, and later—not too much later because you don't want to seem cavalier or uncaring—after you've gotten more information and calmed down, decide if you still want to send it as is. Chances are that you'll want it to be more positive and less defensive.

MOBILE DEVICES: GETTING TO THE POINT

In this age of instant, 24-hour accessibility, it's certainly true that the quantity of our communications has increased. So-called smart phones—Treos, iPhones, and BlackBerrys—and other technologies make it possible for us to ask questions of or reply to our clients or prospects at any time of day on any day of the week.

The *quality* of our communications, however, is suffering. We've become a text-message culture in which abbreviations, acronyms, emoticons, and terse replies—typed haphazardly while in meetings or on the road—serve as poor substitutes for fully formed thoughts.

As a general rule, brevity and economy of language are critical in e-mails because no one wants to scroll through an endless on-screen message. However, this is even more of an immutable law with text messaging and mobile communications. Not only do you have to consider the fact that the recipient doesn't want to read a rambling message, but you also must weigh the tedious personal burden of having to tap out a lengthy note using keypad buttons or touch-screen icons not much bigger than grains of rice.

So, then, is it possible to compose a brief, meaningful text message from a mobile device without resorting to lazy shortcuts? Yes, if you're willing to take a few seconds to organize your thoughts before you start jabbing at the keys.

Use Text in Strategic Spots

If political campaigns can be described as extended sales pitches, then the election of Barack Obama to the U.S. presidency in 2008 provides a useful example of the power of text messaging. The Obama campaign had great success in convincing volunteers and donors—many of them young adults who live and breathe via their cell phones—to register their phone numbers so that they could receive text messages about important campaign news and announcements. These messages, of course, served another purpose: They also asked recipients to support the cause with time or money.

The key here is that these citizens opted into the program. The lesson: Text messages can have a huge impact, but they should be used only with your audience's permission. If you have a database of prospects' phone numbers and are mulling the idea of firing off a quick text message to introduce yourself, think again.

Cold contacting via text isn't prohibited by the U.S. government's CAN-SPAM Act as long as it's sent from a verifiable mobile phone number and not an e-mail address. Coming from an unknown person, however, a text message—no matter how friendly or brief—very well could anger your prospect. In some ways, it's even more invasive than cold calling the prospect by phone because, on the phone, you at least have a few seconds to explain who you are and why you're calling and to establish rapport.

Your best move is to initiate contact with a prospect via letter or e-mail and then follow up with a phone call. Finally, once you've established a relationship with that prospect, you're within your rights to send the occasional text message during the negotiation process.

To gauge a prospect's acceptance of text messaging, be proactive: In one of your first e-mails, grant him or her permission to text *you* with any questions or concerns at any time. And ask politely about whether it's okay for you to send text, and within what parameters. If the prospect knows that you encourage that mode of communication, it may convince that person to send you a text message first, which then opens the door for you to do the same.

Boil It Down . . . Way Down

Text messaging presents the ultimate communication challenge for many sales pros and entrepreneurs, especially those who are comfortable spending hours schmoozing face to face. No other form of contact forces you to distill your message to this extent. It's almost like sales haiku.

Bob, got your message.
Deal looks good re: your concerns.
Watch for details soon.

Believe it or not, within the stingy character-count restraints of many text-message screens, it's still possible to communicate an idea and a benefit effectively—even if you're ostensibly just giving the prospect a straightforward answer to a question. Your mission is to cut to the message's essential parts. Even the preceding semiserious haiku example has its own structure, paraphrased here:

Core idea: The deal looks good.
Client benefit: Your concerns are being addressed.
Call to action: Expect to hear from me; I'll follow up soon.

Because text messaging likely won't enter into your correspondence until you're fairly deep in the sales process, focus on using it as a tool to convey important updates or news during negotiations.

The instantaneous nature of text messaging makes it a good option when you want to communicate something urgent or timely—an answer from management on a sticky negotiation point, for example.

> Answer from HQ: Good to go on $100K (contract length not negotiable). We're within your budget. Expect details by tomorrow.

Don't, however, let the text message serve as your final word on a particular subject. Consider it to be just a quick bulletin before getting into more depth later—it's like skimming the day's headlines on your smart phone at work and then reading the full news stories online or in the newspaper when you get home. If you're out in the field and you've just zapped a message to a prospect on your latest offer, make sure that you follow up with a more detailed e-mail as soon as you're able.

Remember Your Role

So you and the prospect are going back and forth via text. Before you get the urge to fire off a sloppy but quick response to an incoming question, stop and remember your role. Again, you're not a teen planning a Friday night mall run;

you're a professional representing your company. Your writing should reflect that, no matter which device you're using to express it.

On this note, we all use shortcuts when sending text messages because it's just too much of a pain to fully type out our thoughts. In a business conversation, though, you should take an extra measure of care. Use IM (instant-message) abbreviations only if you've got a strong ongoing relationship with a client, and even then, don't overdo it.

If you feel compelled to use a phrase such as *by the way* or *in my opinion,* it's generally better to take a few seconds to type it fully instead of using *BTW* or *IMO,* respectively. (While I've never been a fan of clichés such as *FYI* and *ASAP,* they're acceptable as standard business abbreviations in all circumstances.) More important, if you find that you're bumping up against mandated character limits, go back and delete anything that seems nonessential to the main point (namely, phrases such as *by the way* and *in my opinion*).

Finally—and this should go without saying—if you ever use *OMG* or *LOL* in any client correspondence, regardless of how well you know the person, you should be taken outside and flogged with your BlackBerry Storm.

First, Acknowledge

If you're out of the office and don't have the time to respond thoughtfully to an e-mail or text message from a client, remember this simple rule: Acknowledge, and then follow up. Take 30 seconds to type this from your mobile device:

> Saw your question. On the road today. Will follow up with you tomorrow.

Of course, you'll need to create a reminder to actually follow up. If it's urgent, forward the message to an assistant or colleague (assuming that you have one), and copy the sender with this note:

> Saw your question. On the road today. My assistant Chris will follow up.

Then make it a point to call your assistant to discuss how to track down the answer.

Give It Context

I can't tell you how many times I've e-mailed a colleague or client with a fairly in-depth question that I believed deserved a thoughtful reply, only to receive a cryptic yes or no in response, with no context whatsoever. I'd be left wondering exactly what that yes or no referred to in my multipart query.

Then I'd notice the telltale signature at the bottom: "Sent from my iPhone" or "Sent from my Treo handheld." My colleague was out of the office and couldn't be bothered to give an answer suited to the question. It's a common, hair-trigger response, just to get the reply out of the way. Avoid it unless you're actually responding to a short, simple yes-or-no question. Give your reply a point of reference so that the recipient doesn't have to scroll through the conversation string to figure out what you're referring to.

You might want to follow an example from the world of media training. When a public figure is taught how to respond effectively to an interview question, one of the first things he or she learns is to start each answer by rephrasing the question. This is done so that if the interview is edited in such a way that the questions are never heard, the interviewee's answers will appear as fully formed stand-alone thoughts.

Let's say, for example, that you're in a meeting and you get an e-mail from a client who writes:

> Hi Karen, it's Dave. I've taken a look at your offer sheet, and I have a quick question. Does this include a project management fee, and if so, does it include management of the various subcontractors?

You lower your cell phone under the table and begin to discreetly tap out a reply. Instead of simply typing, "Yes," thus leaving the prospect confused about which part of the question you're referring to, take a few extra seconds to give it context.

> Hi Dave. At a meeting. Re: Offer: Yes, management fee is included along with subcontractor fee. Will follow up later.

Chapter 5

Writing for Each Sales Stage

You've written a great introductory note, and it's helped you to get a foot in the door. What happens immediately after that? It all depends on you and your phone skills. Let's presuppose that you—like any good, high-producing sales pro—have followed up on the letter. You've called the prospect directly and attempted to get a face-to-face appointment.

If the prospect adamantly refuses to see you in person, you've got your work cut out for you. While you're on the phone, be sure to ask the questions that can help you to determine why he or she doesn't want to see you. Then—assuming that this prospect is valuable enough for you to continue sending pitch letters—go back and rework your initial approach to better reflect the prospect's specific needs.

This chapter begins with the premise that you've actually had your first face-to-face meeting with the prospect or at least managed to have a favorable conversation by phone. You've established a personal connection, and now you're ready to begin regular communications.

In the introduction to this book, I stated that a printed letter is a good door opener and that most of your correspondence afterwards will be via e-mail. Thus the examples given in this chapter, apart from the thank-you note, are constructed as e-mail messages. (Later, in Chapter 7, I switch the format of some of these situational messages from e-mail to printed letters. It's your call about which one you feel is most appropriate.)

No matter where you are in the sales process, each message should have its own specific objective related to advancing the discussion to the next phase. Understand, however, that e-mails are no substitute for face-to-face or even phone contact. As you know, you can tell a great deal about how a negotiation is going by observing a person's body language, tone of voice, and overall emotional state. As a "flat" medium, e-mail is severely limited on this front, and it clearly isn't as spontaneous as an in-person conversation. So it should never be used as a stand-alone communication method. E-mail is best put to strategic use as a clarification device or as a follow-up to phone or face-to-face conversations.

Finally, remember that the purpose of this book isn't to teach sales skills. In this chapter you won't encounter the mystical sword in the stone when it comes to one-on-one negotiating or handling objections. Instead, you'll find some tactical tips on how to communicate effectively through writing in every situation you might encounter throughout the selling process.

THE CURRENT CUSTOMER

Prospecting doesn't necessarily mean that you're selling to strangers. Your best opportunities are in fact right under your nose, in the form of your current customers. These individuals or organizations may be loyal purchasers of a particular product or service, and you've built up solid relationships with them over time. Why not approach them about new or incremental offerings?

Send a note thanking the customer for his or her business, and include a "did you know" moment that leads into your introduction of a new product or service.

Subject: A new beverage opportunity from XYZ

Dear Stan:

For the past three years, you've relied on XYZ Distributors for alcoholic beverage delivery to your convenience stores. In return for our timely service and unmatched quality control, you've given us your loyal business, and we truly appreciate it.

Did you know that beyond XYZ's vast variety of alcoholic beverages, we've expanded into the fast-growing category of energy drinks? As a valued customer, you now have the opportunity to carry best-selling Wow-X Energy Drinks from Acme Foods. Based on current sales projections from comparable markets, it promises to be a huge hit with your younger customers.

In the technology world, there's a term *killer app,* meaning a computer program or application so important that it outweighs the value of the larger platform on which it appears. It's your mission to take a new product or service from your company and define it as the killer app for your existing customers. It doesn't have to be tech-related, of course. It just needs to be innovative.

Subject: New breakthrough Acme training solution

Dear Alice:

As a dedicated customer of Acme Executive Services, you know the value of training your leadership team through seminars run by Acme's award-winning pros.

Now, Acme is introducing a revolutionary training system that will forever change the way you prepare your management team for success. Our new iExec Virtual Seminars are interactive online sessions that allow your regional executives to experience all the expertise and insight of our veteran instructors without the expense or hassle of travel.

THE REFERRAL

Aside from your current customer, the referral is the most valuable prospect of all. As you might imagine, the way to go here is to lead with the connection. Make an attempt to tie your own presumably strong relationship with the referrer to that of the prospect's. This gives you an instant sort of common ground. Then seamlessly shift to the business at hand.

> **Subject:** Referral from Ellen Smith
>
> Dear Sean:
>
> I'm writing to introduce myself--I'm a friend and former colleague of Ellen Smith. She suggested that I get in touch with you because she told me that you're in the market for a new home in the Whatsit City area. I happen to be a licensed real estate agent for the award-winning Soldit Realty Co., which covers that region. If you're like me, you listen to Ellen's wise advice . . . so I'm contacting you to find out how I might be able to help in your search.

As a courtesy, send a copy to the person who referred you. Similarly, don't underestimate the power of the casual name drop. Let's say that you're at a networking event or industry affair and you happen to meet one of your prospect's coworkers. You might want to slip that colleague's name into your note—it sends a subtle message that you're making the rounds and that the prospect needs to meet with you to stay in the loop. (As long as you don't imply that you and the colleague are close, you're within your rights to drop the name.)

THE TAKEOVER

If you're new to a sales organization or you're taking over a new territory, the existing customers are also new to you, so you need to make a formal introduction. You can pave the way with a friendly written greeting.

If you know for a fact that a certain customer is loyal and had a good experience dealing with the previous account manager, then make sure that your message is reassuring and establishes your credentials. If you've uncovered any connection or common ground with the prospect, mention it up front.

Subject: Hello from your new XYZ account manager

Dear Fred:

I'm writing to introduce myself as your new account manager. The team here at XYZ, Inc., has told me quite a bit about how dedicated you are to working with us. I can assure you that we will continue to deliver the same high level of customer service that you've come to expect. (On a personal note, I understand that you worked with Susan Jones a while back--she's a good friend of mine.)

Just a quick overview of my background: I have been in the software field for four years and have particular expertise in dealing with the applications that your company uses on a daily basis.

I'd love to set up an appointment to find out how I can help you further achieve your workforce management objectives. (We'll keep things brief because you already know the full XYZ story!) I will follow up by phone to work out a convenient time for you.

Again, Fred, thanks for being a loyal customer. I look forward to meeting you.

If, on the other hand, the customer had a bad experience dealing with the previous representative, you need to stress a new approach. Instead of promising more of the same, address the problem and offer to fix it. In the preceding example e-mail, the first paragraph might be expanded to read as follows:

> Dear Fred:
>
> I'm writing to introduce myself as your new account manager. The team here at XYZ, Inc., has told me that you are a dedicated customer. I intend to make your interests a priority, and I look forward to working with you.
>
> On that note, I understand that you had serious concerns about the customer service provided by the previous representative. I would like to set up an appointment with you to address those issues and to work toward a new approach that will be more in line with your standards for quality and service. We'll keep the meeting brief because I will focus strictly on the issues of your concern.

Note the mention that the face-to-face meeting will be brief. This customer doesn't need a full presentation of your product or service, just the new developments.

THE FORMER CUSTOMER

In terms of prospecting, next in line after the current customer is the *former* customer. This customer has done business with you—or at least your company—before, and while the relationship is now dormant, it's your responsibility to find out why and bring that customer back into the fold.

Let's assume that you've tracked down this person and had a phone conversation in which you've determined why the partnership ended. Maybe he or she had a bad experience with you or another sales representative at your company. Maybe he or she wasn't satisfied with the product quality or the level of support. Maybe he or she was lured away by an irresistible offer from a competitor.

As a follow-up to your phone call and prior to any face-to-face meeting, send a note that expresses empathy for the customer's concerns. Summarize any new developments that might help change the customer's perception of your company, and try to open the door to further talks.

Subject: Important changes at Acme

Dear Margaret:

Thanks so much for sharing your comments regarding Acme Corp. I appreciate your concerns about the quality of our widgets, and I further understand why this would lead you to try a different supplier.

As I mentioned, in the year since you last worked with us, we have undertaken an extensive review and overhaul of our quality-control procedures. We also have strengthened our warranty terms and technical support services.

Based on the changes that I have outlined, how does this affect your perception of Acme? You told me that you are satisfied with the arrangement you have with your current supplier. What would need to happen for you to consider working with us again?

I will call you to discuss the next steps.

Sometimes it's just not possible to call or meet former customers before making written contact—so their specific motivation for severing the partnership remains unclear. In these cases, present your benefits as you would with new prospects, and remind them about why it's in their best interests to come back. Send an introductory letter that includes a mention of the recipient's status as a former customer (e.g., "I certainly hope that your earlier experience with us lived up to expectations.").

THE RIGHT DECISION MAKER

Prospect lists, as you're probably aware, are not always the most reliable source for determining which person in an organization has the authority to make the final purchase decision. Chances are that after sending out a number of introductory letters and then following up, you'll discover that some of those prospects are only part of their organization's decision-making process or in fact have very little to do with it.

To move the sale along, you'll probably need to do what is called *horizontal* and *vertical selling*—connecting with other key players such as an operations manager, a financial director, or a purchasing executive.

Let's say that in following up on your opening letter you've determined that Pete Jenkins, your initial contact, is a manager who can make a recommendation internally, but he'll need sign-off from his regional director to get the deal done. Ask him for permission to contact that person. Then send an introductory e-mail to the decision maker. When you do so, be sure to praise Pete—you want to make him look good, and you want to show the big boss that you're following the proper protocol.

Subject: Following up on Pete Jenkins meeting

Dear Anne:

My name is Joe Smith; I'm the regional sales representative for XYZ Energy Systems. I just had a very productive meeting with Pete Jenkins, your plant manager, who was extremely helpful and clear in outlining your operation's power-generation system needs and requirements. I mentioned that XYZ's ZipTech gas-delivery system could very well be the safe, reliable, and cost-effective solution that your firm has been seeking.

Pete told me that he would like to address this topic with regional management and that you are the person responsible for making purchase decisions on power generation.

> With Pete's permission, I am writing to find out what you think our next steps should be. I have attached a .pdf of our spec sheet, and I will follow up with you by phone later this week. Thanks for reading, Anne.

Note the use of the open-ended statement in the last paragraph. You're not simply asking if you can meet with her, which would require a yes or no answer. Instead, you're leading her into a more thoughtful response. You can ask for the meeting when you follow up by phone.

Don't forget to copy Pete in this e-mail to his supervisor.

THE FOLLOW-UP

How you respond to the initial face-to-face meeting is critical. When you send your follow-up e-mail, use it as an opportunity to advance the conversation to the next stage. If possible, send it within 24 hours of the meeting.

Use the face-to-face meeting as a barometer of where to go next. You might find that the prospect has already bought into the value of your product or service and is ready to see a proposal or even offer you the business (Why can't all prospects be like this?). If this is the case, skip right to "The Solution" later in this chapter.

In most cases, however, now is not the time to ask for the order or even to present a point-by-point solution—you're buying some time to develop that. Instead, here's what you should try to accomplish with this note and how to do it:

- Further the relationship by leading with an anecdote from the meeting or by referencing some other interesting detail.
- Reinforce your positioning by summarizing the prospect's key challenges and how you generally might address them.
- Ask open-ended questions to further engage the buyer and keep things moving.

Subject: Following up on our June 4th meeting

Dear Matt:

It's Dave Doe from XYZ Engineering. I appreciate your taking the time to meet with me yesterday. And thanks for offering your tips on the follow-through to my swing--let's hope it cures me of my tendency to hook it left!

Once we started talking shop, you mentioned that the biggest challenges you face this year are finding the right manufacturer to fit your complex data-acquisition needs, getting more performance out of those instruments with a reduced budget, and minimizing downtime for any new installation. Those issues are what we considered when developing XYZ's latest data-acquisition devices. They've got an easy rollout, they employ state-of-the-art technologies that fit virtually any application, and they're available through a number of flexible pricing plans.

Right now, I have just a couple more questions for you: What else would you like to know about XYZ to help you decide if we're right for you? And if you're at liberty to say, what kind of budget are you working with?

I've enjoyed our discussion so far, and I'm looking forward to continuing it.

Conversely, let's say that after your meeting, you've determined that this particular business isn't worth pursuing because of a minuscule budget or for any other reason. (You probably could have avoided this through sharper list targeting or asking better precall questions, but that's a different story.) Send a simple, considerate note thanking the prospect for his or her time.

> Thanks for taking the time to meet with me today. I truly appreciate your time and your honest feedback regarding your technology needs. In looking at your situation, I think you would agree that XYZ Tech's products are specifically designed for a much larger-scale enterprise than your firm. While it's not feasible for us to work together at this time, please consider us as a high-quality solution should your data needs grow in the future.

THE DEMO

No matter what you're selling or what business you're in, you can make a huge impact on your prospects by helping them to visualize the quality and value that you deliver. It's the old principle of "show, don't tell." If you're selling hard goods, this might mean a visually compelling demo of your product's abilities. If you're selling a service, it might be a vivid description of how a key customer puts your expertise to beneficial use.

Thanks to the Web, you no longer need to do these visualizations in person. If you've got a video camera and simple editing software, you can shoot it digitally, upload it to YouTube or another online video service, and share it with potential customers.

Consider shooting a product demo, case study, or customer testimonial. Keep it short: 90 seconds or less, if possible. Then, after you've posted it online, send prospects an e-mail with a link to the video.

One note of caution: Unless you know what you're doing, you might want to get a professional's help with scripting, shooting, and editing. While various software programs make it easier than ever to cut a video, you run the risk of completely undercutting your message if you put forth a sloppy, amateurish production.

Here's an example of an e-mail with a video link:

Subject: Follow-up from mtg.: Acme demo

Dear Bob:

Thanks again for meeting with me. I appreciate your honest feedback on some of the issues you've been having with your widget suppliers. As I mentioned, Acme widgets have a lab-proven fail rate of less than 0.02 percent.

You had some specific questions about our patented gear mechanism. I could tell you here about how the process works. But I thought it would be much more helpful if I literally showed you how it works and how well it holds up under extraordinary circumstances. I have posted a brief video for you here:

www.youtube.com/cfnjff345

After watching it, please let me know how this kind of performance and reliability might fit with your overall widget strategy.

THE GUEST EXPERT

The prospect has asked you a difficult question about your product or service, one for which you simply don't have an answer off the top of your head. You'd never make something up . . . right? No, you'd do the smart thing. Taking your cue from the courtroom, you'd submit the testimony of a guest expert—a person who either works for your company or serves as a consultant to your industry. He or she could be an engineer or a product-development leader, a marketing professional, a researcher, or any other specialist who gets paid to know even more about the product than you do.

Even if this source is from your organization, his or her statement likely will be afforded a higher measure of weight by the prospect. After all, it's coming not from you, the salesperson, but from a slightly more impartial observer.

If possible, be as specific with the expert's statement as you can, even to the point of presenting it as a verbatim quote. Don't just write

> Good news: My product-development team tells me that the widget can be delivered to your specs within 30 days of the order.

Instead, try

> Good news: Today I spoke to Tim Smith, our director of product development, who said, "We can deliver the widget to Steve's specs within 30 days of the order."

The simple act of putting quote marks around that direct testimony gives the statement more credibility and power.

THE BULLETIN

If at some point during the sales process you come across a bit of news about the prospect or his or her industry that you feel may have some impact on the decision making, then use it as the hook for a new e-mail. It could be an article in a business publication or trade journal, a posting on an industry news Web site, or something from any other information outlet. Use it only if the source is credible.

After presenting a quote from the material and/or a link to it on the Web, ask the prospect point-blank how it will affect the larger conversation.

Subject: Article on Whosit Corp. in Widget Week

Dear Sam:

I just read an article in the latest Widget Week about the closing of your parts factory in Whatzitville. I particularly noted where your COO said that your other facilities are not expected to increase output to compensate. While I'm guessing that you've already seen this, I wanted to pass along a link to the article on the Web, just in case:

www.widgetmonthly.com/whositclosing

In our discussion last week, you mentioned that my company's capacity to service high-volume output is a critical factor in our ability to work together. Now that we're talking about four facilities instead of five, how will that affect your decision making?

THE SOLUTION

Now that you've gotten as much feedback as possible from the prospect, it's time to develop and present your specific solution. When delivering it, you're better off doing so in person. This allows you to get all the key decision makers in the room, break out the laptop for a show-and-tell, get immediate feedback, and gauge the audience's response.

However, a face-to-face presentation may not be feasible, for any number of reasons. In that case, prepare a detailed proposal, and send it with a cover note. You could send it by e-mail (with a .pdf attachment), or you could send a physical document by mail or messenger (this is one of those occasions in the middle of the sales process in which you could opt for a printed letter). If you're fortunate enough to present in person, you'll still need to send a follow-up e-mail summarizing the presentation.

I won't cover the solutions document or presentation here (that could fill its own book), but I will offer a few tips on the cover note. Start by recapping the customer's key business challenges. You can make this as broad or as targeted as necessary based on the level of input you've gotten. Then briefly describe your solutions, point by point. Make sure that you connect them to specific benefits from the customer's world—the more quantifiable, the better.

Here's an example of an e-mail cover note:

Subject: XYZ, Inc., proposal

Dear Janet:

Thanks so much for giving XYZ, Inc., the opportunity to bid on the widget contract. We are looking forward to helping you grow and optimize your operations in the coming fiscal year and beyond. I have attached our full proposal; below is a summary of the main points.

As we understand it, the main challenges facing Whosit Corp. regarding its widget operations are

* An overextended budget owing to unanticipated inventory costs
* Customer demands for faster order processing
* Loss of productivity owing to equipment slowdowns and repair

To help you meet these needs, XYZ can offer

* A two-year contract to supply 4,000 units per year of our award-winning Super3000 Widgets--proven to increase processing speed by 20%
* Three proprietary backup systems, one for each of your facilities, designed to keep the line running in case of primary equipment failure

---

> * A full two-year warranty covering all maintenance and repair, significantly reducing your service costs
>
> Please review and let me know if you have any questions or comments. I will follow up within the next two business days to determine next steps.

THE ASK

You've established value for your product or service, you've met with the ultimate decision maker, you've posed all the right questions, and you've presented your solutions. Now it's time—finally—to ask for the business.

After the prospect has had a suitable amount of time to review your proposal, follow up with a note restating the offer. Then try to nail down a commitment.

You might be wondering about the wisdom of volunteering specific financial figures if the buyer hasn't given you a budget. It's a tenet of the old school of negotiation, in which you never show your cards first. That thinking is a bit outmoded in the modern sales world, however, because you have most likely predetermined a high, middle, and bottom-line value for your offering. By starting high and then making small concessions ideally to get to the middle/high range, you're still effectively in command.

> **Subject:** Next steps between Acme and XYZ
>
> Dear Nicole:
>
> Thanks so much for reviewing our proposal. And again, I appreciate your feedback regarding the challenges you face with inventory control.

I am excited about the possibility of helping you solve these issues through cost-effective Web-based applications.

We have covered a lot of ground over the past few months, and I feel that we have developed a package of solutions that carefully addresses your budget and scale requirements.

To recap, the team at XYZ is pleased to offer you a two-year service and installation agreement for Super5000 inventory software at $36,000, including 24-hour technical support.

Based on your review of the full offer sheet, where do we stand in terms of gaining an agreement in principle? If you have any questions at all, I'm here to help.

THE NEGOTIATION

So the offer is on the table. Now comes the balancing act: getting to a point at which both parties feel that they have achieved their ultimate objectives. The buyer is negotiating for what he or she perceives to be a fair value for your products or services; you're negotiating for what you feel is a fair margin on the value of those products or services.

Sending e-mails during the negotiation phase is especially tricky. Again, there's no substitute for being able to observe a person's body language and tone of voice during this crucial stage, so you shouldn't let the process play out solely in writing. But e-mails are essential for establishing a record of what's been agreed to and what is still up for discussion. And if these messages are written effectively, they can strengthen your position in subtle but important ways.

Whenever you reach a new milestone in your phone or face-to-face negotiations, follow up with an e-mail that clarifies and advances the discussion. Some general rules:

1. Don't give the prospect an opportunity to shut you down with a simple no. Keep your questions open enough to draw out a more meaningful response and to maintain an ongoing dialogue.

> To sum up, we're prepared to offer our full suite of public relations services for a monthly retainer of $7,000, including four hours per month of media training. Based on the wide range of communications needs you've outlined in our discussions, how does this proposal fit in with your expectations?

2. When the prospect makes a blanket statement as an attempt to gain leverage, don't let it go without asking for more detail. Use your follow-up e-mail as another opportunity to dig for his or her true motivations. You'll often uncover something that allows you to shift the dialogue back to more favorable ground.

> You mentioned that our competitors are offering more for the money. Without discussing specific numbers, of course, can you tell me what makes theirs a better deal? I'd just like to ensure that we're making a direct comparison in quality, service, and value.

3. Don't go in with the mind-set that you're going to hammer home one specific solution regardless of what the buyer tells you. Be flexible. If you've hit a dead end in your discussions and it's obvious that the prospect cannot or will not buy in, bring up an alternative solution that better fits his or her needs.

> I understand that your budget won't cover this. So let's look at some other ideas. If, instead of the new model, we went with the certified, refurbished model A540 at $750 per unit and picked up the extended warranty, how might that affect your budget concerns?

4. Always give the perception that the buyer is in control—that the idea is his or hers, not yours. Following up on the example from point 3, let's say that the prospect has picked up on your suggestion and has offered some new twist on it. It doesn't really matter whose idea it was originally; it's his or hers now.

> Just to recap our meeting: You mentioned that you'd like to see a proposal for a combination of repairs and overhauls in your lower-volume facilities, along with the refurbished A540 in your priority centers. A great idea--we should be able to generate a significant savings this way.

5. Sometimes a cliché holds an undeniable truth, as with this dusty one: Negotiation is a two-way street. If you agree to a concession, ask for something of fair value in return, from a larger-volume order to an earlier or extended time commitment.

> We can certainly look at an additional 10% discount. It's something that we offer to customers who commit to 300 units or more per month. If

> that isn't feasible, we could look at alternative arrangements, such as moving up the start of our contract period to October 1.

6. Compliment the buyer on his or her negotiating prowess, and communicate that you understand where he or she is coming from. This is a good lead-in for a response to a particularly tough demand.

> I appreciate the fact that you're doing everything to maximize the value for your company. I'd do the same thing in your position. On your point about the added-value program, we certainly can look at extending it, with the understanding that my firm offers that option exclusively for commitments of two years or more.

7. If you're getting close, but still no deal, introduce sweeteners that add the perception of value but don't cost your side much in real terms. This could be anything from an extended service guarantee to added insurance.

> If we were to extend your free 24-hour tech-support period from 12 to 18 months, how might that affect your thinking on this?

8. Recognize that your prospect is likely to be only part of the decision-making process. Even if you've convinced him or her, the odds are

that he or she still will need to sell the idea to his or her own upper management. Give the prospect everything he or she needs to do it.

> I'm glad we've reached an agreement on the basic terms. However, I know you still need to run this past Jim. What else can I provide to make sure that you have everything you need for that conversation?

THE OBJECTION

What's a negotiation without an objection? Some sales pros and entrepreneurs relish a moment like this because it gives them an opportunity to prove their own worth and that of their product or service. (And they understand, rightfully, that an objection is actually a confirmation of interest on the part of the prospect.)

Others dread it, out of fear that they don't have the "right" response. In determining how to handle it in writing, it's helpful to look at what could happen during a face-to-face negotiation.

You've likely been sitting across from a prospect when he or she raises a specific objection. You counter tactfully. Then he or she dismisses your point in a semiantagonistic way. You restate your case, a bit more firmly, but it only increases the tension. Soon, the exchange has deteriorated into a heated, emotional debate that puts the whole deal at risk.

Now imagine this exchange occurring through e-mail. As I've mentioned, e-mail is no place in which to judge the sender's emotional state or intentions. When dealing with objections via e-mail, even the simplest declarative statement from the prospect can be misinterpreted as a dig against you or your company.

It's important to never let an objection-focused e-mail conversation drag on beyond a couple of messages from each party. If you've presented your counterpoint via a pair of e-mails and the client continues to shoot venom back through your in-box, end it right there. Pick up the phone or, better yet, get yourself in front of that person. Effective writing can do a lot of things, but when tensions start to escalate, there's simply no substitute for face-to-face resolution.

That said, here are some things to keep in mind when handling objections in writing. First, make no judgments, and don't let your emotions get the best of you. Instead, find common ground by expressing your understanding of how the prospect feels. State your case, and ask questions to keep the conversation going.

> I understand completely. If I had heard negative things about a company's reputation, I'd think twice about working with them. I did want to mention that new management has been in place for the past six months and has instituted a number of changes. Customer feedback has been positive. Assuming that the comments you've heard are based on older perceptions and given the changes I've mentioned, how might we proceed from here?

The most common objection is, "You're too expensive." When you get this one, explain the value of what you offer and how your product or service will save the customer money in the long run. Make sure to support your claims with quantifiable evidence.

> I can understand that cost would be a major concern--it's an issue for everyone in our field. That's why XYZ Corp. has made a decision to focus on long-term value. An independent lab study found that XYZ widgets run for an average of 5,000 hours without replacement. That equals a per-hour operational cost of $2--a small price to pay for such a critical function. How might this information factor into your thoughts on cost?

Similarly, if the prospect tells you that he or she is working with another provider and doesn't think that it's necessary to switch, remind him or her about what he or she deserves from a supplier—and how you offer more of it.

> I respect the commitment that you have to your current vendor. At the same time, I think that you'd agree that it's critical to get an optimal level of performance out of your suppliers. Acme ensures this by delivering an extended warranty, 24-hour tech support, and industry-leading capacity. How might this factor into a decision to look at other options down the road?

If, early in the process, the prospect tells you, "We just don't have any need for your services," bring up a secondary need, if it exists.

> I can certainly appreciate that. One quick observation: Your Web site mentions that you have operations in Southeast Asia. We have products specifically for those markets. Can you let me know how that might affect your needs?

A related tip: If the prospect says that he or she doesn't need your services "right now," ask him or her, "When might I be able to check in to see if the timing is better?" Better still, let the prospect know that you will think about alternative solutions and that you'd like to set up another meeting to discuss them.

THE GOOD NEWS

You just won a big customer-service award. Your company is offering a limited-time deal. Your firm just landed a big contract with an influential client that could help sway others in the industry.

It's easy to bang out this message, right? Not necessarily. Watch out for pitfalls: Don't go off on a tangent about it, and don't forget to reinforce your core positioning.

Most important, don't forget to apply the "so what" test: How does this specific bit of news benefit the client? Even if the benefit is seemingly obvious, try to go beyond a surface explanation and get the client to see the longer-term positives.

For example, if you're announcing an exclusive financial offer, it's tempting to leave it at this:

> We're prepared to lock in your rate at just $2,500 per month on a four-year contract. You'll be saving 20% off our standard rate.

Announcing the savings rate is good; giving it context is better, such as

> We're prepared to lock in your rate at just $2,500 per month on a four-year contract. That's 20% off our standard rate--making a real difference when you're faced with the rising operational costs in our industry.

Even better is justifying a rate decrease in positive terms. Some clients might look at a rate cut or special offer as a sign of diminished value. It's your responsibility to position it by explaining the positive circumstances that brought it about.

Acme has improved its internal efficiencies to the highest level yet, thus enabling us to pass on savings to select customers like you. As a result, we're prepared to lock in your rate at just $2,500 per month on a four-year contract. That's 20% off our standard rate--making a real difference when you're faced with the rising operational costs in our industry.

THE BAD NEWS

Then there's the e-mail that no one wants to send: the bad news. You just had a recall of the product you're trying to sell. You sent a proposal with the wrong numbers. You promised that you could deliver some feature or benefit, but you misspoke.

Instead of letting it jeopardize the deal, however, look at it as an opportunity to become the hero—provided you take the right steps to correct it.

Be honest about any glitches or mistakes. Customers have a funny way of finding out about these things, so trying to ignore or cover up a blunder will only make the situation worse. Also be prepared to accept responsibility even if someone else in your organization screwed up. You can yell and scream all you want behind the scenes, but the prospect doesn't want to hear you blaming the person in the production department. Besides, admitting a mistake goes a long way toward building trust.

After reading the news, the buyer probably will fume for a bit. But if your response is measured and proactive enough, cooler heads will prevail eventually, and you will be able to get the process back to where it should be.

You've got three choices in your approach:

1.   You can buy yourself some time to figure out what to do.

Dear Joan:

I wanted to give you an important update. In speaking to Jack Smith, brand manager for Super500 software, I have confirmed that the application is in fact not compatible with your current platform. Based on what I saw in the product specs, I had told you that it was compatible. So I take full responsibility for the mixup.

I have three priorities right now. First, I will figure out why and how this happened on my end. I also will work up an alternative solution with as little financial impact on our offer as possible. Finally, I will put a better system in place to make sure that this never happens again. How does that sound?

Thanks for your understanding; I will follow up with you as soon as possible.

2. You can put the ball in the prospect's court. The second paragraph might read:

We will, of course, need to revise the offer and look at another solution. Ideally, what would you like to see done to fix this?

3. Or you can immediately suggest a specific fix. The second paragraph might read:

> Management agrees with me that the best solution is to offer you a 15% discount on the licensing agreement to cover the costs of upgrading to the newer platform. We also will assist in sourcing and installing the new system. How does that idea work for you?

Regardless of which approach you choose, admit the problem, take responsibility, and ask an open-ended question to prevent the conversation from shuddering to a halt. When you present your solution, expect the prospect's response to trigger a new subset of negotiations.

THE NUDGE

If the prospect is dragging his or her feet on a decision or has disappeared at a sensitive stage of the negotiation, send a quick e-mail asking where things stand. If you have to, copy the prospect's management or another key purchasing decision maker within his or her organization. Then follow up with a phone call shortly afterwards.

> **Subject:** Status on Acme deal
>
> Dear Anthony:
>
> Since it's been one week since our last meeting, I wanted to follow up to find out where we are regarding Acme's server solutions. You had mentioned that you needed to upgrade your current system prior to the fourth quarter. We are now approaching a critical date in terms of whether we can achieve the installation to your data center requirements.

I have provided pricing, specs, and a service agreement (attached again here for your convenience). Can you please let me know what else you need to make your decision at this point?

Thanks for your consideration.

THE CLOSE

Now it's the moment of truth. You've done everything imaginable to get this business. You've answered every objection that the buyer has raised, you've negotiated in good faith, and you've moved toward compromise wherever possible. But you're still getting either the traditional pushback or the old runaround. Enough. It's time to close this thing or walk away.

When you're presenting your final offer—the point at which it makes no business sense for you to offer further concessions—explain your position clearly and carefully, and then ask for the order one last time. Summarize the offer as briefly as you can, preferably using bullet points. You can attach a deadline to the offer as long as you give a valid explanation (i.e., production schedules).

Subject: Final offer from Whatsit Corp.

Dear Mark:

Thanks for passing along the latest feedback from your team. Following discussions with Jason Smith, Whatsit Corp.'s president, and Susan Jones, our VP of sales, we have agreed to the following:

* We will reduce the per-unit price from $8.25 to $8.00.
* We are asking for a contract extension from 24 to 26 months.
* Total order: 26,000 units.
* We will extend technical support to cover the additional two months free.

This is our best and final offer. We feel that it provides the most effective combination of value and flexibility for your firm. Based on this fit with your business objectives, do we have an agreement?

This offer is valid until 5:00 p.m. on April 10, which is the deadline for production. I would hope that we can speak with each other before then, but if we haven't gotten a response by that point, we'll have to assume that the deal is off the table.

I will follow up by phone to confirm that you've received this e-mail.

THE WALK-AWAY

Part of your role as a sales pro or entrepreneur is to know when it's time to move on—time to abandon a clearly unproductive negotiation and turn your resources and energy toward a different prospect that represents a better fit with your products or services.

Walking away from the table when you've reached a hopeless deadlock is an extremely difficult thing to do, especially when you've invested a lot to get to that point, but it's sometimes necessary. After a meeting in which it's been determined that both parties are too far apart to continue any meaningful discussion, follow up with an e-mail that summarizes the conversation. Be sure to copy your management.

The e-mail should restate your position and thank the prospect for his or her time. Most important, if you've determined that there may be a glimmer of hope for the future, in which a changed circumstance or two could crack the door open again, emphasize that.

Subject: Recap of March 18th meeting

Dear Scott:

I'm writing to follow up on our last meeting. Following is a summary of the final offer from XYZ Manufacturing:

* 250 units @ $400/each
* Commitment deadline of March 31
* Order delivery date of June 30
* Two-year extended warranty

Your executive team has determined that this offer is still too far outside your budgetary and scheduling requirements to be practical. However, you also have mentioned that your company will reevaluate its widget operations in the next fiscal year. Meanwhile, I have promised to further address the subject of delivery deadlines with XYZ's product team.

Both parties have agreed that it does not make sense to continue discussions this fiscal year. While I would love to have your business, I am also responsible for maintaining the worth of XYZ's products and services, and to compromise further would jeopardize the value of our business.

Thank you for the time you've devoted to this process. I appreciate your professionalism and dedication to the value of your business as well.

I will follow up with you in the fall to discuss alternative solutions.

THE COMMITMENT

Naturally, because you've used your interpersonal skills so effectively on your sales calls—and because you've heeded the principles discussed in this book—you won't need to walk away. You'll instead be on the receiving end of the four sweetest words that any sales pro or entrepreneur can hear: *"We've got a deal."*

Congratulations. After all those weeks or months of hard work, you've finally come to an informal agreement with the buyer. All that's left now is for you to deliver the contract for signature and kick off the celebration. Send a brief confirmation e-mail outlining the terms one last time, express your gratitude, and offer a hopeful, forward-looking statement about the partnership. Copy all the major players from both parties.

Subject: XYZ and Whatzit partnership

Dear Emily:

On behalf of everyone here at Whatzit Industries, I am very grateful for your business. It's an exciting day for us because we're all looking forward to launching this partnership and helping your business achieve the growth it deserves.

This is to confirm that we have agreed in principle to the following:

* 2,000 widgets @ $300/each
* Order delivery date of May 25
* Two-year extended warranty

I will send over a contract for your signature. Please let me know if you have any questions. Again, we truly appreciate your decision to place your trust in us. We will do everything in our power to exceed your expectations.

THE THANK-YOU NOTE

The contract has been signed, hands have been shaken, and pats on the back have been proffered by management. Pop the champagne cork—you've officially won the business!

Following the face-to-face meeting that cements the deal, your first act is to send the perfect thank-you note to your new client. While you've probably been e-mailing back and forth with the buyer for weeks or months leading up to this momentous occasion, now is not the time to send just another e-mail.

This moment deserves something a bit more personal. A printed—or even hand-written—thank-you letter on high-quality paper stock represents both a physical and symbolic token of your new partnership.

You can get a little personal, showing a bit more emotion than you might in regular business correspondence. (While I'm usually not big on exclamation points, feel free to go for it here.)

A nice gift enclosed with your letter doesn't hurt either. Be careful with this, however, because some companies have rules about the maximum value of gifts—you want to avoid the appearance that you've "bought" the business. If you've confirmed that your new client is allowed to accept a gift, your best bet is to give something that aligns with his or her personal interests (which you've ascertained during the sales process). Or you simply could buy lunch.

Dear Carol:

Thanks so much for your business! I'm looking forward to being your go-to person for whatever questions or requests you may have during our partnership.

It's been a long process getting to this point, but throughout it all, I have appreciated your fairness, honesty, and professionalism.

So now, before we begin to roll out the installation, it's time to relax. On that note . . . I know you're a fan of spa treatments, so please accept the enclosed collection of Naturala Spa products to enjoy at home, with my compliments.

THE ONGOING RELATIONSHIP

Since the focus of this book is limited to the period between prospecting and the close, I won't go into a lot of detail about ongoing communications with your new client. But I will offer a few general tips.

You've been proactive throughout the sales process, so you should be even more hands-on now that you've won the business. Here are a few ways you can keep on the client's radar during your partnership:

- Shoot a quick e-mail if you spot anything that might affect your client's business or well-being—new technologies, market opportunities, or trends.
- Send a message asking whether the client is getting orders or services delivered in a timely, reliable fashion and whether he or she is satisfied with your customer service.
- Inform and educate about new product or service offerings from your organization—this is an ideal opportunity to build incremental business.
- Every so often, send a simple, creative note that says, essentially, "Thank you for your ongoing business." It's an unexpected gesture that any client will appreciate.
- Finally, take advantage of the fact that a satisfied client is your best stepping stone to new business. After a suitable amount of time in which you've demonstrated strong follow-up and customer service, ask the customer for a (nonconflicting) referral. Make sure to offer something in exchange.

Subject: Thanks . . . and a question for you

Dear Bill:

Thank you for the partnership that we've built over the past year. I think we can both agree that our collaboration has exceeded expectations on both sides.

I trust your judgment, and I recognize that an endorsement from you carries a great deal of weight in our industry. So I'm hoping you might be able to offer the name of a friend or colleague who potentially could benefit from my services. (This would be a contact noncompetitive with your business, of course.) With your permission, I would like to mention our connection in any message I send to this contact.

Likewise, please know that should you ever need a personal reference that attests to your character and honesty, I will be the first in line to offer one.

Chapter 6

The Cheat Sheet:
An English Refresher

You're fired up and ready to go out and sell. You are definitely not in the mood to hear about spelling or grammar, which is why you probably took one look at this chapter title and rolled your eyes. But hang in here for a moment.

If you're like most salespeople or entrepreneurs, you haven't given a whole lot of consideration to proper language usage in your letters and e-mails. You've got more important things to worry about than whether you used the word *its* correctly.

However, by maintaining proper form, you'll gain a subtle advantage over the competition. Amid the piles of poorly written e-mails received by your prospect on a daily basis, your error-free message will set you apart from the typo-ridden pack.

To put it another way, proper form is a key measure of professionalism. With that said, here's a quick (I promise) overview of everything you need to know about spelling and grammar without having to go back to school.

SPELLING

Wellcome to my all-tyme pet peev in the wurld of bisnes comunicatons. As someone who works with words, I find my heart sinking every time I come across a letter or e-mail strewn with so many misspellings that I need a decoder to get through it. Misspelled words have the uncanny ability to turn a powerful letter into a shoddy mess and to make you and your company seem less than professional. The cry of "I can't spell!" is *not* a valid excuse for mangled words showing up in your sales communications. We all make mistakes, but this is one of the most easily avoidable.

How much you learned in school about spelling is something only you and your English teacher know, so we won't get into spelling lessons here. Instead, here are two words for you: *spell check*. Any letter or e-mail sent without being screened by your word processor's spell-check program is flirting with disaster. Especially since most word processing programs automatically display a red line under questionably spelled words on the screen, there's really no excuse.

That said, your spell-checker should be taken with a fat grain of salt. It's far from comprehensive or infallible. For example, a spell-checker can't tell you that you spelled the client's name or company name wrong. If you've committed that unpardonable sin, all your credibility goes out the window. Your prospect's name (and, if applicable, company, title, and address) should be typed while looking at the person's business card or should be lifted directly from a reputable client database, the prospect's Web site, or an e-mail signature. If that's not possible, call (or have an assistant call) to confirm the information.

A spell-checker also may not be familiar with your industry jargon or be up-to-date enough to keep up with ever-changing tech or business lingo. (My spell-checker remarkably still flags such words as *blog* and *Google*, for example.) If you can use other sources—trusted industry journals or Web sites—to get definitive, confirmed spellings of new or unusual terms, manually add them to your spell-checker's dictionary so that you have them covered in the future.

Finally, a spell-checker cannot tell you that you used *it's* instead of *its* or *there* when you meant *they're*. (Meet another of my pet peeves.) For these crucial grammatical elements, refer to a good dictionary (see below for suggestions on reference tools), and take a look at the grammar and usage guidelines in this chapter.

Reference Tools: Thesaurus and Dictionary

Just because you're not a writer by trade it doesn't mean that you shouldn't invest in a set of writer's tools. Get yourself the latest edition of *Webster's Collegiate Dictionary*. Or, if you don't want to make the investment, just bookmark Dictionary.com on the Web. Then use it on a regular basis. If you're not absolutely sure of the spelling or meaning of a specific word, take 30 seconds to look it up.

You also should vary your word choices by picking up a copy of *Roget's Thesaurus* or at least bookmarking Thesaurus.com on the Web. Use this resource carefully, however. As I mentioned earlier, it's not your job to impress clients with your vocabulary. Do not break open the thesaurus simply to pull out complex words and sprinkle them throughout your letter or e-mail. You'll come across as pretentious or, if you misuse any of those big words, foolish.

Instead, hit the thesaurus if you find yourself using the same descriptive terms over and over. For example, if you're selling to the luxury market, don't keep using the term *luxurious* to describe your offerings—it gets monotonous. The thesaurus can give you some fresh alternatives: *lavish, majestic, upscale,* etc.

Proofreading Takes Five Minutes

Perhaps the most important rule of all: Take a few minutes to proofread your own letter or e-mail line by line. Most of us don't have the budget to hire a professional proofreader for our communications, but if you have an assistant, give him or her the opportunity to look at them as well. A second set of eyes has a better chance of catching things that you may have missed.

COMMON GRAMMATICAL MISTAKES

Misspellings are unforgivable in a sales letter; grammatical errors are only slightly less so. The vast majority of business communicators suffer small lapses in grammar here and there—I'm certainly guilty of it. Chances are that if your letter contains a minor glitch or two, no one is going to notice it. It's when the errors start piling up like a chain-reaction highway wreck that your writing comes off as second-rate.

Following are general guidelines for avoiding common mistakes in grammar and usage. Refer to them if you're ever unsure about proper form. But don't obsess over the rules or let them overwhelm your main sales message. You don't necessarily want to sacrifice impact on the altar of proper form.

Affect/Effect

Affect is a verb; *effect* is a noun.

> This development will profoundly *affect* the way you do business.

> This development will have a profound *effect* on the way you do business.

The exception: *Effect* should be used as a verb only in this context: To *effect* a change means "to bring about a change."

> Beginning June 1, we will *effect* a change in our return policy.

Among/Between

Between refers to the relationship of two things; *among* refers to more than two things.

> The competition is *between* Acme Corp. and XYZ, Inc.

> The competition is *among* Acme Corp., XYZ, Inc., and Jones Corp.

Assure/Ensure/Insure

Assure means "to put a person's mind at ease about something" ("I *assure* you that . . ."); *ensure* means "to make certain in general" ("I want to *ensure* that . . ."); *insure* means "to provide money in case of loss" ("We will *insure* you against . . .").

Complement/Compliment

Complement means "to complete or round out."

> This new widget *complements* our current product mix.

Compliment is what you do when your client gets a new hairstyle.

Continuous/Continual

Continuous means "ongoing, without interruption or break."

> Our fuels go through a *continuous* distillation process.

Continual means "ongoing, but only at frequent intervals."

> We are *continually* making improvements to our product line.

Good/Well

Good is an adjective. *Well*, by itself, is an adverb. When you're referring to an abstract verb such as *feel*, use the adjective.

Yes	No
I feel good.	I feel well.
I feel bad.	I feel badly.
I see well.	I see good.

On a related note, if you write, "Our company is doing well," it means that your company has had a good year financially. If you write, "Our company is doing good," it means your company is contributing to socially responsible causes.

I/Me

If you're referring to yourself and another person and you're not sure whether to use *I* or *me*, here's an easy way to remember: Mentally remove the other person's name from the sentence and see if it still makes sense.

Wrong:
John and me will meet with you. (Me will meet with you?)
Right:
John and I will meet with you. (I will meet with you.)
Wrong:
You'll be meeting with John and I. (You'll be meeting with I?)
Right:
You'll be meeting with John and me. (You'll be meeting with me.)

When you're part of the object of the sentence, as in the second example above, always list the other person first, as opposed to "me and John." It's not just proper grammar; it's good manners.

Its/It's

Among grammatical mistakes, this one is the big enchilada. Here's the deal: *Its* is possessive, like *her* or *his*. Use *it's* only as the abbreviated version (contraction) of *it has*.

It's been a long time since our competitor lived up to *its* promises.

Any time you get the urge to write *it's,* imagine substituting *it is* in your sentence: "Our competitor did not live up to *it is* promises." Doesn't make sense? That's because the proper usage is *its,* not *it's.*

Regardless

Don't be one of those people who says, "Irregardless of this development. . . ." *Irregardless* is not a real word. (It's an erroneous combination of *regardless* and *irrespective,* two words that mean basically the same thing.) For the record, *regardless* means "in spite of" or "without consideration to."

Than/Then

Than is used to indicate a relationship between two things.

> Their price is higher *than* ours. Our price is less *than* theirs.

Then is used to indicate a transition in a sequence of events.

> First, we'll set up a meeting; then we'll work out a strategy.

That/Which

As a preposition connecting two parts of a sentence (see "Prepositions" later in this chapter), the general rule is to use *that. Which* should be used when you're setting off a clause with a comma, and the phrase that follows is nonessential.

Wrong:

I would like to discuss the proposal which I sent you.

Right:

I would like to discuss the proposal that I sent you.

Also right:

I would like to discuss the latest proposal, which I sent you last week.

There/Their/They're

Simple:

> *There* is a place. (We will go *there*.)
>
> *Their* is a possessive. (We discussed *their* plans.)
>
> *They're* is a contraction of *they are*. (*They're* planning for next year.)

Who/Whom

Whom is dying out, thankfully, because it's so confusing, and it has a tendency to make sentences sound stuffy. For now, the simplest rule is this: Use *whom* after such words as *to, for, from, with, around,* and *about* (see "Prepositions" on the following page). Other than that, use *who*. Examples:

> . . . for *whom* the bell tolls.
>
> . . . to *whom* I owe a great debt.
>
> Jim Doe is a man *who* has had great success throughout his career.

Whose/Who's

Whose is a possessive. It should be followed by a noun (or an adjective and then a noun).

> XYZ Corp. is a company *whose* goals are far-reaching.

Who's is a contraction of *who is.* It should be followed by a verb (or an adverb and then a verb).

> Susan is a person *who's* going places.

Your/You're

Your is a possessive. It should be followed by a noun (or an adjective and then a noun).

> When *your* financial future is at stake, turn to XYZ Corp.

You're is a contraction of *you are.* It should be followed by a verb (or an adverb and then a verb).

> With XYZ Corp., *you're* getting the highest quality.

USAGE AND FORM
Prepositions

A preposition is a word such as *on, at, for, through,* or *across* that links a noun to the rest of the sentence. In the sentence, "Dave sat at the table," the word *at* is a preposition linking the subject (Dave) to the object (table). English teachers and other purists might tell you that you can never end a sentence with a preposition.

> That's the subject I'm referring to.

Technically, the correct way to say this is

> That's the subject to which I'm referring.

The rules of business are more relaxed than those of academia. Use your judgment: If your grammatically correct sentence comes off as though written by a nineteenth-century schoolmarm, drop the *whom* and use the less formal structure.

Some mistakes, though, are worse than others. Here are a couple of awkward ones:

> CPAs are the audience we are developing the product for.

> Who is this story by?

Rewriting the preceding sentences using proper grammar would make them sound clumsy, however, so just simplify them.

> We are developing the product for CPAs.

> Who wrote this story?

Singular versus Plural Nouns: Data/Media

Here's another rule that's dying out. People so often use the terms *data* and *media* incorrectly that when someone actually uses them the correct way (as plural nouns), it almost sounds strange. For the record, it's "The media *are* . . ." and "These data *are*. . . ."

Few will notice if you make *data* a singular noun ("This data *is* . . ."), so don't sweat it too much. As for *media*, you'll sound more professional if you use it correctly as a plural noun. If you want to talk about, say, the Internet, TV, or newspapers alone as a specific field, it's a *medium*. If you forget the rule about *media*, mentally substitute *press outlets* for *media*.

Numbers

Generally, you should write out all numbers under 10 (i.e., *one, two, three, . . . , seven, eight, nine*) within the text of your letter or e-mail. With any number higher than nine, you should use numerals. Feel free to relax the rules for promotional purposes such as taglines and product names.

Regardless of the number, you should never start a sentence with a numeral. If you want to begin a sentence by saying, "2008 was a challenging year for our industry," for example, rewrite it as follows:

> Our industry had a challenging year in 2008.

And unless it's in a bullet point, don't start a sentence with "50 percent of our customers. . . ." It's "Fifty percent. . . ." For hints about how to present numbers to your best advantage, see Chapter 3.

Verb Tenses

Lessons about verb tenses could fill their own book, so I won't go into a long explanation here. The one thing that you should remember is that if you write something like, "We worked very hard to get to this point," it sounds as though you worked in the past and now you've stopped. If you write, "We *have worked* very hard to get to this point," it sounds like it's ongoing. And in many cases, this is the effect you're trying to achieve.

Subject/Verb Agreement

Wrong:
Our family of satisfied customers are . . .
Right:
Our family of satisfied customers is . . .
Wrong:
The average donor gives an hour of their time.
Right:
The average donor gives an hour of his or her time.
Also right:
On average, donors give an hour of their time.

The verb should agree with the subject regardless of any clauses that come after the subject. The simplest way to remember this is to mentally remove any clause that begins with modifiers such as *of, in, for, about,* and *around* or any clause set off by commas. In the first example above, mentally remove the clause "of satisfied customers" to get "Our family is. . . ."

Note: Family is always singular noun, as is *audience, group, collection*, and *pair*, so the verb that comes afterwards should be singular (*is, was,* etc.).

For the purposes of grammar, refer to a company or organization as a thing (singular noun), not as a group of people.

Wrong:
Acme Corp. has met their financial projections.
Right:
Acme Corp. has met *its* financial projections.

Parallel Construction in Lists

When listing sales points in a paragraph or when using bullet points, make sure that you keep the same construction for each point. Don't write:

In the past year, our company has

- Won several major accounts
- 40 percent increase in sales
- Expansion into new markets

Be consistent by using a series of past tense verbs, for example:

In the past year, our company has

- Won several major accounts
- Increased sales by 40 percent
- Expanded into new markets

On that note, you're always better off using action-oriented verbs (e.g., *won, increased, expanded,* etc.) in your lists (see Chapter 3 for more).

Word Order

Misplaced words or phrases in sentences cause confusion—and your reader doesn't have the time to read them twice.

Wrong:

> Acme Corp. produces inventory software for the small-business owner that reduces time-to-market and cuts costs.

Huh? Is the small-business owner the one who reduces time-to-market and cuts costs?

Better:

> Acme Corp. produces inventory software that reduces time-to-market and cuts costs for small-business owners.

or

> For small-business owners, Acme Corp. produces inventory software that reduces time-to-market and cuts costs.

Possessives/Apostrophes

For most nouns, it's simple: to make them possessive, just add *'s*. Examples:

Charles's assistant will contact you.
The boss's office is impressive.
The princess's crown shines.

If you're referring to plural nouns as a possessive, tack on an apostrophe at the end. Examples:

Our companies' sales projections are due soon. (Referring to several companies)
The agents' clients have signed their contracts. (Referring to several agents)

Two notable exceptions to this rule are *man's* and *woman's*—both plural nouns that require *'s*.

If you're mentioning a family name that ends in *s*, add *es* when referring to the members of the family as a group. Add an apostrophe only if you're referring to a possessive. Examples:

We've been keeping up with the Joneses. (Family name is Jones.)
The Rosses' business is going strong. (Family name is Ross.)

Hyphens

Use hyphens when you're using at least two words in a row to modify a noun. Examples:

the slow-moving vehicle
the up-and-down stock market

The exception is if the first word is an adverb that ends in *ly*. Then you don't need a hyphen. Examples:

a wholly owned subsidiary
a carefully crafted proposal

If you're using a lengthy phrase to modify a noun, add hyphens throughout the modifying phrase. Optionally, you can set off the phrase with quotation marks.

> We don't buy into the whole "today's-youth-don't-care-about-the-future" argument.

Colon versus Semicolon versus Comma

A colon is a device you can use if you're about to explain something and you want to build some drama leading up to it. It is in some ways interchangeable with the em dash (—) or ellipsis (. . .), which are covered in Chapter 3.

> XYZ Corp. has seen remarkable growth in sales: up 30 percent in the first quarter.

A semicolon should be used to separate related points. You use it in place of a comma if the new clause is a full sentence *or* if you're separating several clauses that already have commas in them.

> Many customers of XYZ Corp. use our convenient online ordering; others order from our extensive catalog.

163

> XYZ Corp. makes copiers for small, medium, or large businesses; printers for commercial, residential, or institutional use; and scanners for a variety of uses.

A comma should be used to separate words or simple clauses, not full sentences. (Because of the word *whereas* below, the last part of the sentence is a clause.)

> Most customers of XYZ Corp. order via online, whereas some order from our extensive catalog.

A comma added before the word *and* in a list of three or more (e.g., "online, catalog, and retail stores") is called a *serial comma*. It's employed in this book; it's your call about whether to use it in your writing. (Just be consistent in your choice.)

Quotation Marks/Punctuation

When using a direct quote, the punctuation usually goes inside the close quote. If you're mentioning the source at the end of the quote, include a comma inside the close quote.

> "The new product from Acme Corp. is a winner," says the *Whatsit Post*.

On that note, try to avoid long direct quotes in your letters. It's the same principle as discussed under "Let Your Customers Sell for You" in Chapter 3.

If you've gotten a favorable but lengthy testimonial or press quote, don't quote it verbatim. Pull out the most relevant parts, and splice them together with ellipses.

> "The new product from Acme Corp. is ingeniously designed . . . and shows great promise for the future," says *Machinery Week*.

If you feel compelled to include a long direct quote, don't wait until the end of the quote to reveal who said it. Particularly if it's a big media source or a well-known name within the industry, you want the name to appear right away. Look for a logical break in the first sentence, drop the source in there, and continue with the quote.

> "The new product from Acme Corp. is ingeniously designed," says *Machinery Week*, "and shows great promise for the future. It represents the dawn of a new era in data processing."

Redundancy

Avoid	Use
absolutely essential	essential
past history	past *or* history
end result	result
basic fundamentals	basics
still remain(s)	remain(s)
minimum requirements	requirements

Clichés

Business-language clichés come and go so rapidly that it's nearly impossible to compile a list of tired, overused phrases to avoid in your correspondence. Use your judgment: If half the people in your office are constantly throwing around such terms as *think outside the box, that ship has sailed, moving forward, at the end of the day, paradigm shift, the net-net is, the bottom line is,* or *we're ramping up for it,* it's a good idea to erase them from your memory permanently (the phrases, not necessarily your coworkers).

Mixed Metaphors

Where clichés lurk, mixed metaphors often follow. A *metaphor* is a language device that directly compares the subject of the sentence with something seemingly unrelated (e.g., "Our sales manager hit all the right notes in that meeting today" or "The deal almost crashed on the rocks, but she steered it back on course"). In the former, the sales manager is compared with a singer; in the latter, the deal is compared with a sailboat.

A *mixed* metaphor occurs when the sentence brings in *two* references that are completely unrelated to each other. Changing the second example above to, "The deal almost crashed on the rocks, but she made a game-saving catch," turns it into a mixed metaphor because it combines a sailing reference with a baseball reference. When you're trafficking in metaphors, make sure that all parts of the statement make sense in combination. Better yet, avoid tired analogies such as these altogether.

Economy of Language

Get to the point. Don't use three or four words when you can use one or two.

Instead of	Try
During the time that . . .	While . . .
Owing to the fact that . . .	Because . . .
For the reason that . . .	For . . .
In the event that . . .	If . . .

It is possible that we might . . .	We may . . .
It has come to my attention that . . .	I noticed that . . .
Please accept my thanks . . .	Thanks . . .
I want to thank you . . .	Thank you . . .

Stretching the Rules

Expanding on my earlier comment that you shouldn't obsess over the rules, this is an appropriate time to note that certain rules were meant to be broken. Never mind what your teachers told you: Feel free to start sentences with *And, But,* or *Because.* Some strict rules of grammar need to be loosened for emotional impact.

> XYZ Corp. is changing the rules of personal finance. And we'll change the way you think about retirement, too.

Similarly, feel free to use sentence fragments.

> When choosing an insurance company, consider the things you find most important. Your loved ones. Your health. Your home.

Use this technique for a more conversational tone. But, as with everything else, do not overuse.

Sample Letters

In bite-size pieces of information throughout this book, you've seen the many ways in which you can use written language effectively to help close a deal. Now it's time to put it all together.

This chapter offers dozens of sample letters and e-mails that incorporate many of the book's concepts. You'll find complete messages representing every major stage of the sales process.

Please note that these are samples, not generic templates. I recommend against copying them verbatim and plugging in your company's information. For one thing, I've attempted to make them more realistic by putting them in the context of a variety of real industries and sales categories, which means that a vast majority of the fields presented won't have much in common with yours.

More important, if you were merely to copy the letters from top to bottom, you'd be ignoring the single most vital element of a sales note: your own personality. As I mentioned in the introduction, your mission is to communicate in your own voice. You already exhibit your own distinct style and tone in phone calls and face-to-face meetings; you should do the same in your letters. So use these sample notes for inspiration, not imitation.

Finally, I'll take one last opportunity to remind you that your letters and e-mails should be more than the sum of their parts. If you attempt to stuff every writing tip into a single sales note, you'll render the message unreadable. Instead, draw on the techniques that feel most natural to you and have the most relevance to your business. Save the rest for the right tactical opportunity down the road. And if appropriate, get a trusted colleague to review your note for overall clarity and adherence to your brand message.

Good luck—and happy selling!

The Cold-Call Letter: Examples

Dear Advertising Professional:

If you're like most marketers, you've been forced to make some difficult decisions about how and where to spend your advertising dollars. Because the volume of ad spending is hard to come by, it's time to focus on efficiency—namely, making sure you're getting maximum results from your leaner budget.

I'm writing to let you know that one media group is committed to helping you maximize efficiency: the LocalBiz Regional Network. As the largest, most influential print and online information source for businesses in the Midwest, we cater to decision makers—the people who can make a critical difference in sales and awareness for your brand.

That efficiency begins with the environment that surrounds your ad message. From cover to cover and throughout our Web sites, we feature exclusive, expert information that builds trust for each of our marketing partners. Our content includes

- The trends that will shape the regional economy for years to come
- The deals that are transforming the business landscape
- The opinions that influence the legislative environment

Who's reading this valuable content? Your target audience. LocalBiz print editions are distributed to 50,000 top managers—that's 1 out of every 6 such managers in the region. Meanwhile, our Web sites receive 40,000 unique users per month. You'll be relieved to know that there's no need to spread valuable advertising resources elsewhere.

Finally, wouldn't you want assurance that a publication's readers are motivated to act on your message? We deliver it. According to our most recent subscriber study, 58% of our readers said that they have visited a Web site or called an 800 number as a result of reading an ad in our publications.

Please take a look at the enclosed sample copy of *Whatzitville Business*, our flagship publication. I will follow up with you by phone to discuss some ideas about how you can achieve the advertising efficiency your brand deserves.

Regards,

MyName

P.S.: We're helping advertisers in a tough economy. In our Year in Review edition, we're reducing our regular four-color rates by 25%. The closing date is October 19; please contact me at myname@localbiznet.com for more details.

Source: XYZ Circulation Report; LocalBiz Subscriber Study

encl.

Want More from Your Supplier? Look to an Aero Plus Award Winner.

Dear Ben:

The fast-moving changes in our industry mean that you're likely frustrated by unpredictable standards in quality and service in the supply chain. Fortunately, one company consistently fulfills its clients' needs: Soar-X Corp. We're the all-in-one supplier for the aerospace field, with a wide variety of high-quality components and engineering solutions, each backed by award-winning service.

Choose the Solution That Fits.

Soar-X delivers both a full range of structural components and integrated avionics for aerospace applications and a wide array of engineering and design services for manufacturers of commercial, military, and business aircraft. Our nearest competitor, on the other hand, offers 25% *fewer* components in its full line. Thanks to the diversity of Soar-X's offerings, you're certain to find the solution that fits your needs and is scaled to your enterprise.

Get More Out of Your Components.

With this unparalleled product depth comes lab-tested quality. The independent XYZ Research Corp. recently determined that the tolerance rate for our aluminum and alloy components is 22% closer than that of our nearest competitor. That equals longer-lasting products, lower repair costs, and less stress for you during budget time.

Find the Right Answers When You Need Them.

Once you take on our components, you'll receive the highest level of customer service during your ownership period. Last year, Soar-X received the Aero Plus Award, one of the industry's highest honors, for our aftermarket service and support. You've got the security of knowing that a dedicated team is responsible for the safety and quality of the systems and processes you acquire from Soar-X.

Ben, if you've been disappointed in the performance of your suppliers, it's time to take a fresh look at what a proven company can do for you. Please review the enclosed Soar-X brochure, which highlights some of our main product categories. And visit us on the Web at www.soar-xlabs.com. I will follow up by phone in the next 10 business days to discuss how you can gain better quality and service from your component provider.

Regards,

MyName

encl.

Dear Ms. Jones:

As a responsible, affluent investor, you face numerous questions about your financial future: How can I maintain cash flow in this market while building retirement income? Should I pull back on my tolerance for risk? How can I preserve my legacy on behalf of my loved ones? You shouldn't have to face these questions on your own. So consider one last question: Is your current financial advisor working hard enough for you?

At Bigwig Financial Advisors, we focus strictly on your distinct financial goals. This personalized attention is why, for more than three decades, we've been a reliable, independent resource for an exclusive group of high-net-worth individuals like you.

In a volatile financial environment, the most precious commodity is trust. Having served investors through bull markets and bear, and today handling nearly $15 billion in assets, our team of experienced professionals has earned the unwavering trust of our clients. In fact, one-half of our clients have been with us for at least five years—an assurance that you're getting long-term wealth management advice.

You deserve a financial strategy as singular as your own life's ambitions. Bigwig will put together a completely personalized plan so that you can achieve your dreams. One of our longtime clients, the owner of a family business, knows this approach firsthand. As he says, "Bigwig worked closely with me to develop a well-balanced portfolio that helps preserve capital, manage risk, and take care of my family's future."

The key to this service is our independence. Bigwig earns no commissions on transactions, so we have no incentive to choose one investment vehicle over another. As a registered financial advisor, our only agenda is to maintain your best interests.

Thank you for reading, Ms. Jones. Please visit our Web site at www.bigwigfinancial.com, and feel free to contact me at 123-456-7890 or myname@bigwigfinancial.com if you have any questions. I will follow up by phone in the next week or two to strategize with you on achieving your personal goals and dreams.

Sincerely,

MyName

P.S.: Bigwig Financial's president, Tom Bigwig, has just been named "Financial Expert of the Year" by *FatCat Finance* magazine . . . another measure of our trustworthy customer service. Isn't that the kind of performance you want from your advisor?

Proof of Painovra's Efficacy: 9 in 10 Patients Would Use It Again.

Dear Dr. Smith:

On a daily basis in your examination room, you see the often-debilitating effects of chronic pain. Your patients may be frustrated after trying certain pain-relief medications and getting little, if any, sustained alleviation.

As an account representative for BigPharmCo, I am writing today to let you know that your patients have a safe, reliable alternative: Painovra DG. Clinically proven to deliver long-lasting relief of pain and associated side effects such as nausea, Painovra comes with industry-leading value-added services, including a proprietary discount program.

Delivering Superior Pain Relief

Based on the results of a recent primary-care study, Painovra generates more effective relief than the largest-volume prescription pain reliever. Isn't that what counts in your practice—and in the day-to-day lives of your patients? Some key findings:

- 91% of Painovra patients said that they would take Painovra again for pain relief.
- 73% reported relief from pain within one hour vs. 43% of patients who took the most commonly prescribed pain reliever.
- 76% were free of pain after 24 hours vs. 46% with the most commonly prescribed medication.

Minimizing Side Effects

As you know, a pain reliever's effectiveness is only as good as its ability to control major side effects. Here, too, Painovra delivers measurable results. In the clinical study, more than 6 in 10 patients who originally reported nausea and then took Painovra experienced relief of nausea after three hours.

Optimizing Patient Support

Finally, because your patients will be grateful for relief from economic stress, BigPharmCo has created a customized program that helps them afford their Painovra prescriptions. By enrolling in the Painovra Plan, patients who refill their prescriptions on a regular basis can save up to $15 per month (restrictions apply). The plan is the latest addition to BigPharmCo's award-winning value-added programs, including 24-hour in-service support and educational services.

Please take a look at the enclosed product sheet, which contains more detail about Painovra's proven efficacy. I will follow up in the next few days to set up a time to discuss your need for pain-relief solutions based on your patient profile.

Dr. Smith, thank you for your time. I look forward to helping you enhance the quality of life for your patients.

Sincerely,

MyName

encl.

Dear Communications Purchasing Manager:

Two years ago, a midsize private hospital in Ohio faced a major challenge: Its ability to share lifesaving information was at risk due to an aging, inadequately scaled communications system. At the same time, it was dealing with budget inefficiencies as it juggled multiple providers. So management turned to a single innovative provider of voice, IP, and data solutions. Today, not only is that facility benefiting from a world-class network, but it also has reduced its communications costs by 40 percent.

I'm sharing this with you because the company that produced these results is the one I work for: ZapCom. By delivering IP telephony as well as converged, mobile, and fixed broadband networking, we help to streamline operations and boost critical efficiencies for midsize companies, particularly health-care organizations like yours. In turn, we help clients to afford their end users a reliable, simple-to-use communications experience.

By working with ZapCom, you'll get a robust network with ever-evolving technologies and applications. Our research and technology team—with combined experience of seven decades in the field—looks far down the road on your behalf to anticipate the next phase of your communications needs. Partner with ZapCom now and help to make your job more manageable in the years to come.

The story of the Ohio hospital is just one example of how the ZapCom network helps to optimize business processes. The independent health-care research firm Smith Associates determined that ZapCom's clients have seen their communications costs decrease by an average of 33% over two years. Think about how that can free you to deal with other vital budget concerns.

Finally, you and I both know that these technologies mean little unless they can help to direct end users to the information they need as quickly and easily as possible. So your physicians, patients, and administrative staff will appreciate ZapCom's three solutions:

- High-volume voice systems—calls get through, no matter how busy it gets.
- Lightning-fast data transfer—information moves fast because lives are on the line.
- Crystal-clear videoconferencing services—in this field, every small detail counts.

For more about how ZapCom's real-world-tested voice, data, and IP solutions can help you to get ahead of your communications challenges, please visit www.zapcomtech.com. And feel free to call me at 123-456-7890 if you have any questions.

Thank you for reading; I will follow up in the next two weeks to discuss the short- and long-term needs of your network.

Best,

MyName

Dear Small-Business Owner:

As a busy entrepreneur, you're adept at wearing many hats: product developer, salesperson, tech troubleshooter, to name a few. However, rapidly changing regulations and business conditions mean that the tax/finance hat is a particularly tough one to wear.

Let a team of skilled professionals handle it for you. Proffit & Lozz Associates is an accounting and financial consulting firm with targeted expertise in small businesses. By working with our veteran CPAs, you'll tap into five decades' worth of combined experience in general accounting and financial analysis so that you can

- **Secure your future.** Proffit & Lozz can deliver financial analysis, including long-range budgeting, forecasting, and projections. As your business changes, you'll be able to manage it. A client of ours, Susan Walker of Walker Florists, says, "P&L was able to help me look several years out. I'm now in a position to achieve responsible growth."
- **Maintain compliance.** The pros at Proffit & Lozz not only will help to ensure financial reporting and tax compliance but also will explain exactly how new regulations affect your specific business. Another of our clients, Bill Smith of SuperCo, knows the value of this service: "When the tax laws changed, P&L made sure that I was ready. I can now focus on bigger-picture issues."
- **Get automated.** You'll be better able to monitor your financial picture when Proffit & Lozz helps you to learn, set up, and manage digital solutions such as Zippster software, voted by the readers of *Small Biz* magazine as the most effective financial software. You'll spend less time tracking your bottom line and more time enhancing it.

To discuss how you can bring your company's accounting structure in line with your long-term business objectives, please contact me at 123-456-7890 or myname@proffit-lozz.com. I look forward to working with you.

Sincerely,

MyName

P.S.: Tax day is less than 13 weeks from today. Are you prepared for what the new laws mean to your business? Call me at 123-456-7890 for a free consultation so that we can strategize to keep you ahead of the game.

Dear Human Resources Professional:

Recently, a large service organization faced a dilemma during its national sales meeting. Owing to a family emergency, the keynote speaker had canceled the day before. The company's management placed a panicked call to its event-planning partners. The pros on the other end of the line stayed calm and made things happen. They found a motivational expert who was free that day, arranged for his travel, and briefed him on the company's needs. All went off without a hitch, and the speaker earned rave reviews.

Which event-management company pulled this off—and regularly helps to save the day for its clients? SuperEventCo. I'm writing to let you know that the team at SuperEventCo is ready to build a customized event strategy for your company and seamlessly handle any new wrinkles along the way. We'll do it all at highly competitive rates, with help from the most respected subcontractors in the field.

Whether planning professional meetings, large-scale conferences, high-visibility product launches, or memorable destination retreats, SuperEventCo has a vast collection of resources at our disposal. So if you need something at the last minute, we'll place the right calls and get it for you. It's just one reason why we received a special commendation from the Regional Chamber of Commerce last year.

In a challenging economic climate, your event budget is a precious commodity—and you can rest assured that we will treat it as such. Sally, a human resources executive at a regional transportation company, had this to say about SuperEventCo's conscientious approach: "We've worked with them several times, and they have always been extremely fair in their estimates and in their final billing."

You're probably also concerned about the quality of subcontractors hired to carry out your company's vision. That's why we work with only the best. For their track record of reliability and creativity, our subcontractors regularly receive top ratings on the BigServiceList consumer ratings Web site.

By spending a few minutes with me on the phone, you'll be on the road to a well-run, cost-efficient, custom-tailored event. Please contact me at 123-456-7890 or myname@supereventco.com at your convenience. And feel free to visit our Web site at www.supereventco.com to read more client success stories.

Best regards,

MyName

P.S.: Just 90 days from now, the holiday season kicks into high gear. Is your company prepared for it? Contact me at 123-456-7890 by August 30 for a complimentary event estimate, and you'll receive 15% off our standard management fee.

Live the Eco-Conscious Life You Crave . . . and Cut Energy Costs by 46% or More.

Dear Roger:

As a supporting member of the Environmental Help Coalition, you understand the importance of achieving energy independence. Using a sustainable energy source for a home or business can take pressure off the earth's dwindling natural resources while boosting economic prospects at a personal and community level.

I'm writing on behalf of Sunupp Energy, which has installed more solar electric systems in the Southwest than any other firm. You now have a forward-looking opportunity to live green and save money with Sunupp's innovative renewable-energy solutions for residential and commercial buildings.

Reduce Your Carbon Emissions

Solar electric systems are a proven solution for a greener future: A recent government study confirms that they produce 85% fewer hydrocarbons than oil heating. Sunupp technologies are designed to perform cleanly for up to 50 years without replacement. By using Sunupp to take your home or business off the electrical grid, you're making a powerful statement about your long-term commitment to the environment.

Generate Long-Term Cost Savings

Imagine life with drastically reduced or nonexistent monthly energy costs. A recent study by the independent Sustainable Power Research Board determined that over the course of 15 years, a Sunupp installation is projected to save an average of 46% on energy costs. Available federal tax credits can save owners even more. That money can go toward the things that matter to you—like contributing to the preservation of our environment.

Rely on Start-to-Finish Support

Do you need to be an engineer or solar expert to make this work for you? Definitely not. In Sunupp Energy, you've got a proactive, full-service partner that will walk you through the process from installation through ongoing analysis and maintenance. You simply enjoy the savings and fulfillment of green living. This approach earned Sunupp the coveted ZipStar Award for Customer Satisfaction last year.

Please take a look at the enclosed brochure, which showcases a variety of Sunupp options for your specific needs, from full solar electric to hybrid systems. Then contact me at 123-456-7890 or myname@sunuppenergy.com for a free consultation and price quote.

Roger, I look forward to helping you get started on the road to energy independence—and all the personal and community benefits it brings.

Sincerely,

MyName

encl.

WorkTime Network Magazine: "Super3000 Software Is Best for Business."

Dear Ron:

When facing increased competition and rapidly evolving technological needs, what would it mean to your organization if you could boost business efficiency by as much as 50%?

I'm writing to give you a privileged look at the solution endorsed by leading retailers and the tech media: Super3000 business automation software from WowTech. By using its wide array of critically acclaimed, enterprise-level systems, you'll boost the speed and efficiency of critical business processes—putting your company in a better position to compete in a tough market.

Filling out spreadsheets and other business documents is tedious and takes employees away from doing the things that really matter to your business, namely, generating revenue. Super3000 software helps staff to complete required tasks (expense reports, purchase requests, time sheets, and order processing, to name a few) almost instantly. In turn, it helps to deliver consistent, transparent reporting results. Our clients have experienced productivity and efficiency gains as high as 50%.

Custom-tailored Super3000 programs from WowTech have been an integral part of the business growth for multinational companies, highly trafficked e-commerce sites, and leading regional retailers such as Acme, XYZ, WowCo, SuperCo, and Bigtime Stores.

And in the past two years alone, our technology has garnered many of the most coveted honors in the tech industry, including

- The *WorkTime Network* magazine Gold Star Award
- The Techie Software and Online Data Expert Awards
- Class-leading 76% user-satisfaction rating from MegaGlobal Research

Ron, this letter only touches the surface of what Super3000 can do for operational speed and efficiency. The best way to experience its award-winning solutions is through a one-on-one demonstration. I will follow up with you next week to show you how the smartest companies are getting leaner, faster, and better positioned for the future. In the meantime, please visit www.super3000solutions.com for more detail on our integrated systems.

Thanks for reading.

Best regards,

MyName

Dear Paula:

Last year, a woman moved to Whatzitville and began comparison shopping local gyms. She was disappointed to find that most were expensive and offered cookie-cutter classes. She visited the largest club last, assuming that it would be more of the same. But she quickly discovered that it specialized in high-quality, personalized training at affordable rates. She signed up and has since lost 25 pounds and markedly boosted her energy level.

Which health club made the difference? WowBody Fitness. Because you're new to town, you have a privileged opportunity to get your own smart deal: Sign up by May 15 and receive a limited-time introductory rate of $45 per month with no initiation fee. A small price for membership at the place where you can achieve measurable results.

At WowBody, you'll find a wide selection of innovative programs, each designed to help you stay fit on a consistent basis. One example: our six-month WowBody Challenge. Last year, members who completed the Challenge reported an average body-fat decrease of 15%, while 70% dropped at least one size in clothes.

You're also assured of working with the most highly trained and respected instructors in town. Each of our personal trainers is certified by the National Federation of Fitness Trainers, and our lead yoga instructor, Sue Jones, won a *Whatzitville Times* reader poll as "Instructor of the Year." Trust them to keep you moving toward your fitness goals.

Right now, you're probably dealing with the challenge of finding services in your new town. I want to make your choice of a new gym hassle-free. Contact me at 123-456-7980 or myname@wowbodyfitness.com by May 15 to join WowBody Fitness at the introductory rate of $45 per month, with no other fees attached. All of us at WowBody look forward to helping you shape your personalized health and fitness program.

Best,

MyName

P.S.: Here's one more reason to get fit with WowBody: When you sign up for 10 personal training sessions, we'll give you 2 free. That's an additional $160 in savings, available to you if you sign up by May 15. Call me at 123-456-7890 to get started.

Dear Danielle:

A recent study in *HR Business Journal* found that companies with at least 30% employee turnover each year are half as likely to be profitable as those with lower turnover. A question for you, then: What is your company's turnover rate? If it's high enough to affect your overall productivity and efficiency, then the time to fix it is now.

The Proven Way to Keep Top Talent

I'm writing to introduce you to the employment solution used by more than 500 savvy companies nationwide: SuperHire Staffing. We combine expert recruiters, innovative technology, and painstaking candidate screening, all in service of helping our clients find—and just as importantly retain—the most valuable talent in the field.

Expert Judgment, Better Candidates

Filling a valuable staff position is too important to leave to chance. The veteran recruiters at SuperHire Staffing have delivered, on average, more than 250 successful placements throughout their careers in diverse corporate environments including health care, technology, insurance, and hospitality. You'll see only the best applicants as a result of our experience and judgment.

Easy Applicant Management

In your day-to-day job, you often need to make decisions quickly—especially when it comes to hiring. So you'll appreciate the convenience of SuperHire's proprietary Applicant Center database. Job candidates are assigned their own secure online area containing résumé, work samples, referrals, and more—giving you all the information you need in one spot. In a recent survey of 100 of our top clients, 4 in 5 said that the Applicant Center had an overall positive effect on their hiring decisions.

High Quality through Meticulous Screening

When job candidates arrive at your office, you want assurance that they've been carefully prequalified. SuperHire helps to ensure the highest-quality applicants—and ultimately, higher retention rates—by requiring each candidate to undergo skills evaluations, personality tests, and a thorough background check. Kelly Thomas, HR director at Acme, Inc., is a client who trusts our system: "When we get a candidate from SuperHire, we know we're getting top talent."

I will follow up with you in the next few days to discuss the latest, most effective strategies for employee retention and how they might help YourCo boost its long-term business prospects. In the meantime, please visit www.superhireco.com to see case studies of some of our most successful client engagements.

Thank you for reading, Danielle. I look forward to speaking with you.

Best,

MyName

Dear Lucy:

Running YourCo's employee benefits program in-house probably means that your hands are full, so I won't take up much of your time. I'm contacting you with the opportunity to shift YourCo's benefits administration from your overburdened team to a group of outside industry experts. At the same time, I want to help you make your employees happier, with more choices and affordable rates.

My company, BigBenefit Advisors, is a full-service employee benefits consultant and broker-age that helps HR groups like yours free up time to focus on other issues that affect day-to-day business operations, all while boosting employees' job satisfaction.

According to a survey in *CorpBenefit Journal*, the top factor in determining whether an employee is happy with a benefit plan is that worker's ability to choose from among several options. BigBenefit can help you to deliver the choices employees want, including

- **Flexible medical plans**—From PPOs to HMOs, your employees can select from an extensive network of local doctors and affordable co-payments.
- **Competitive retirement savings plans**—You'll help to ensure employee loyalty through proven, reliable SEP IRA, 401(k), and other financial options.
- **Substantial disability benefits**—Our short- and long-term plans will help to assure employees that they are covered if the unexpected happens.

Rarely does a benefits plan combine wider choices with all-around lower premiums, yet Big-Benefits does exactly that. Our relationships—we've worked with dozens of respected providers over the past two decades—allow us to negotiate the most affordable rates for your company with the lowest impact on your employees' paychecks.

With this upgrade in services comes a reduction in workload for your team. BigBenefit will handle everything from the enrollment process, to billing administration, to performance analysis. One of our clients, the HR director at a national financial services firm, says, "Big-Benefit serves as an extension of our department. They're true partners."

Please take a look at the enclosed brochure, which outlines BigBenefit's services and how they can make your employee benefits program more effective and easier to administer.

Lucy, thank you for sharing your valuable time. I look forward to helping you craft strategies that reduce the stress on your team and raise the loyalty and satisfaction of your employees.

Best regards,

MyName

encl.

Home Prices Are Down 20% This Year: The Time to Buy Is Now

Dear Value-Focused Renter:

As an apartment renter, you're wisely focused on maximizing your budget. What if you could keep a tight rein on your finances and own a home instead of renting? Home prices are down by 20% in the Tri-County area this year, which means you may never again get this kind of opportunity to find a spacious, high-quality home at a bargain price.

I am prepared to assist you every step of the way. Work with me—an award-winning Realtor from SuperHouse Realty—and you'll realize three advantages that will help you to reach your goal faster:

- A number of safe financial strategies to help you afford your new home
- Unmatched local-market insight and experience
- The largest number of exclusive home listings in the Tri-County region

Get Started on Financing

Mortgage credit is difficult to come by, so if you're concerned about getting a loan, you can get a head start here. Visit www.superhouserealty.com for valuable ideas on securing financing toward the home you deserve. A recent internal survey revealed that 76% of my clients found this resource helpful when planning to buy a home.

Uncover Our Exclusives

You could go to any real estate agency to look at shared listings. By working with SuperHouse Realty, however, you'll find a wealth of home listings available nowhere else. Clients of our nearest competitor, on the other hand, have access to 25% fewer exclusive listings.

Get Inside Knowledge

Finally, you'll benefit from my 14 years of expertise in the local market, which earned me the Tri-County Realtor of the Year Award in 2008. You'll get inside information—from the traffic flow on a certain street to the best dry cleaners in the neighborhood—that will help you to make the most informed decision and ensure satisfaction with your home.

Please visit www.superhouserealty.com for a small sampling of our current listings. Then contact me at myname@superhouserealty.com or 123-456-7890 to schedule a free, no-obligation appointment. We'll begin discussing your specific home-buying needs and brainstorm some ideas for finding you an ideal home in a market ripe with bargains.

Best,

MyName

Dear Greg:

As small-business owners, both you and I know that the scope of our responsibilities far outweighs the length of our workdays. We must take the time to analyze the details of everything from vendor agreements to employment matters while trying to focus on long-term business plans.

I'm writing to let you know that my law firm, Murge & Aguirre Associates (M&A), exists solely to handle these details for you. By partnering with us, you'll access the legal knowledge, flexibility, and dedicated service usually reserved for large corporations that can afford in-house counsel—while gaining more time to spend on business growth.

A Trusted Partner for Local Companies

M&A is the one law firm in the Whatzitville region dedicated to the distinctive needs of small to midsize businesses like yours. For any legal concern that crosses your desk, you can trust in our partners' combined 75 years of experience in general corporate law. M&A's professional services include

- Mergers, acquisitions, and divestitures
- Intellectual property transactions
- Commercial litigation, arbitration, and mediation
- Contract negotiation

Counsel Targeted to Your Business

Most important, these solutions can be custom-tailored to your business. You can engage us on a retainer or flat-fee arrangement because we know that your budget is a major consideration. And you'll know exactly where you stand on any legal issue because M&A explains everything in practical terms that relate to your firm's best interests. According to one of our clients, Tim Jones of ThatCo, "The team at M&A is reliable and professional, and they truly care about the growth of my business."

Please feel free to contact me at 123-456-7890 or myname@murgeaguirrelaw.com or stop by my office for a free consultation.

Greg, thank you for reading. I look forward to answering the legal questions you deal with on a regular basis—so that you can regain focus on what really matters to your business.

Best,

MyName

P.S.: Did you know that according to *SmallBiz Journal*, small-business owners spend an average of 75 hours per year on contracts and other legal matters? Think of what you could be doing with that time. Call M&A at 123-456-7890 to find out more.

The Former Customer: Examples

Subject: Following up on Wow-Med conversation

Dear Kyle:

Great speaking with you yesterday. And thanks for bringing me up to speed on your facility's medical instrumentation needs. To recap, you said that Wow-Med was once your primary source for instruments, but you switched to a direct online supplier two years ago to save time and money.

I want to bring you up to speed on what Wow-Med is doing to help medical office administrators like you. In the past two years, we've not only maintained our status as the supplier of the most reliable medical instruments, but we've also taken significant steps to make our products more affordable and easier to buy.

In a field as critical as yours, quality matters. You already know that Wow-Med sells nothing but precision-engineered surgical instruments. When you order from us, you're getting a product of certified origin, made from the highest-grade stainless steel. A client of ours, Jo Anne Smith of the Whatsit Medical Group, says, "Wow-Med products perform flawlessly every single time. You can't put a price tag on that."

In terms of actual costs, Wow-Med has added a generous volume discount program that can deliver real value when you factor in purchases across your regional network. We've also recently extended what was already the strongest warranty program in the industry: We now cover all repair and maintenance up to 10 years (restrictions apply). Longer product life translates to greater long-term savings.

Just as important, since I arrived at Wow-Med last year, we've completely upgraded our online ordering system to make the process faster, simpler, and more efficient. Spend a minute or two at www.wow-medsupplies.com, and imagine the ease of hassle-free purchasing.

Based on this, how would you feel about scheduling a brief meeting where we can discuss the most effective strategies for your instrument purchases? Looking forward to our conversation.

Best,

MyName

Dear Fran:

Two years ago, you had a singular opportunity to discover the award-winning service and resources of GlobalHop Travel. We hope the memories from your trip are treasured ones and that the experience lived up to your expectations.

I'm writing to let you know that GlobalHop has gotten even better since you last used our services. First, we've earned the Leisure Service Award for the fifth and sixth years in a row—proving that even our industry peers recognize our outstanding customer service. And we've joined the prestigious WorldOver Network, bringing our total number of international travel suppliers to nearly 3,000—giving you more choices and greater value.

Most important, GlobalHop has prepared creative new travel packages, so now is the ideal time to choose your next adventure. Just a couple of options:

- **Caribbean Paradise**—Explore crystalline waters and white-sand beaches. We'll arrange scuba diving, jet skiing, nightclub passes, and more. Book by March 30 for seven days, six nights starting at $699 per person, based on double occupancy.
- **Old World Europe**—Enjoy the extras that we're known for, including museum tickets, winery visits, and countryside tours. Book by March 30 for seven days, six nights starting at $1,499 per person, based on double occupancy.

See our Web site www.globalhoptravel.com for full rates and restrictions.

Whether you're ready for a free one-on-one travel consultation or you have comments or questions about your previous experience with GlobalHop, I'm looking forward to hearing from you. Please contact me at myname@globalhoptravel.com or 123-456-7890. Thanks for reading, Fran.

Best,

MyName

P.S.: Both privileged travel packages I described above must be booked fewer than 60 days from now before rates increase. Contact me at 123-456-7890 to reserve a vacation with maximum amenities and minimal hassle.

The Referral: Examples

Dear Tom:

My name is Dan Jones, and I'm a licensed transportation broker for Truxomatic Corp. A former colleague of mine, Sue Smith from Acme Corp., suggested that I get in touch with you. She said that you two know each other through the Market Trade Association and that you're planning a review of your transportation suppliers for the next fiscal year.

You're probably looking to get more out of your transportation partner in terms of flexibility and reliability—which are the exact qualities that Truxomatic has been delivering to each of its clients for more than 30 years.

It's clear that you have a wide product range—and Truxomatic has the resources to cover it. On your behalf, we select from 10,000 bonded and insured contract carriers with refrigerated trailers, dry vans up to 53 feet, flatbeds, and customized vehicles. (Our nearest competitor, on the other hand, gives its customers 30% fewer carrier options.) No matter the product, you'll get the smartest choice for transporting it.

What really matters is whether your goods get to their destination. That's why we demand strict compliance from our partner carriers in terms of safety, insurance, and experience, and why we employ precise tracking technologies including GPS. For these efforts, Truxomatic has been honored with the Intrastate Customer Service Award and the Truck Safety Gold Medal. This means you can be assured that your goods will arrive in ideal condition. And less damage or fewer losses mean less impact on your finances.

Tom, I encourage you to visit www.truxomatic.com to see how we put all this into action for our clients. And please contact me at 123-456-7890 or dan@truxomatic.com if you have any questions.

Finally, thanks for letting Sue connect the two of us. I will check in with you later this week so that we might discuss some new ways to optimize your transportation plans.

Best regards,

Dan

Dear Larry:

My name is Joe Smith, and I'm VP of sales for Internet consulting firm SuperNetCo. I'm writing at the suggestion of my good friend Janet Thomas, whom you know from the Tri-City Chamber of Commerce. She mentioned that your company is considering an overhaul of its Web strategy, including e-commerce operations.

SuperNetCo's team might be able to help here. After reviewing your site, we've seen where you might be able to streamline the user experience (to get people to the shopping cart faster); we've also thought about some opportunities for revenue-driven marketing strategies.

First, I'm sure you'd like to know a little about us. SuperNetCo serves as a one-stop resource for Web site design, e-commerce development, and strategic marketing, which spares our clients the time and expense of juggling multiple vendors.

Like you, we're businesspeople first. We also happen to know Web technology inside and out. This combination has translated into a solid record of product launches and redesigns, online ad campaigns, e-commerce rollouts, and more. A client of ours, Bill Smith of Acme, Inc., sums it up: "With SuperNetCo, I feel as if I'm working with peers who really understand my objectives."

And we benchmark our success on our clients' measurable growth in Web traffic and revenue. One example: A large online retailer reported a 34% upswing in sales within six months of reconfiguring its e-commerce platform with our help.

Thanks for reading, Larry. Please visit www.supernetco1.com for samples of our work, and feel free to contact Janet directly if you'd like to hear her valuable opinion about my own standards of performance and service.

I will follow up in the next few days to brainstorm some ideas about optimizing your firm's Web operations.

Best,

Joe

The Takeover: Examples

Subject: Hello from your new WideRock Insurance agent

Dear Ted:

I'm writing to introduce myself--I'm your new agent at WideRock Insurance. Thank you for your loyalty as a customer over the past several years. You've come to expect top-tier service, product selection, and flexibility, all of which have made WideRock one of the best-regarded insurance companies in the country.

Know that I will do everything in my power to exceed those standards during our partnership. I have spent the past four years at a national life insurance provider, where I was known as a respected, dependable problem-solver for my clients. You can read comments from several of my customers at www.widerockinsurance.com; just search for my name.

You've already made the wise decision to establish a long-term care policy for you and your spouse--helping to ensure that you will be able to afford outstanding care at a nursing home or assisted-living facility or at your own home. My responsibility is to see that you have peace of mind in all aspects of your life, so I will call you in the next two weeks to discuss your overall insurance strategy. (I promise to keep this brief because you already have a good understanding of the company itself.)

Again, Ted, I appreciate your dedication to WideRock. I look forward to helping you strengthen your financial security and enhance your quality of life.

Best regards,

Tammy

Subject: Greetings from your new Commuterrific rep

Dear Ashley:

I'm writing to introduce myself as your new account representative at Commuterrific Outdoor Media. My role is to help clients like you build creative advertising solutions that deliver brand exposure to the widest audience possible.

In speaking to the management team here, I understand that you had some concerns with the service of the previous account representative assigned to you. You can be assured that I take the issue of service very seriously.

I am moving over from the digital division of Commuteriffic's parent company, where I worked as a true partner with clients—helping them to plan campaign strategies, monitor results, and keep a tight rein on quality control. Take a look at the November issue of *Digital Ad Solutions Monthly*, in which a customer called me "a true pro who goes above and beyond for us."

Thank you, Ashley, for your honest feedback. You deserve an account representative who places a high priority on your specific interests, and I intend to do exactly that.

I will call you in the next few days; I'm hoping that we can plan a quick face-to-face conversation that focuses on the most effective ad strategy for your brand.

Best,

MyName

The Current Customer: Examples

The New Sleekster RS Is "a Revolutionary Vehicle"—National News Network

Dear Christine:

As the owner of a Trident LS, you appreciate how economical and reassuring it is to drive an Accelera vehicle. Did you know that Accelera is about to introduce a sedan that raises its award-winning standards of safety and fuel efficiency to an even higher level . . . and that Township Motors has one waiting for you at a preferred rate?

With your lease term ending in six months, now is the ideal time to stop into Township Motors for a privileged first look at the new Sleekster RS, which, in a recent preview report, was praised by National News Network as "a revolutionary vehicle that could transform the auto industry."

Class-Leading Safety

Thanks to its patented new Safe-T Airbag System, the Sleekster was independently lab-proven to deliver 30% more injury protection than other vehicles in its class—so you can rest easy knowing that you and your loved ones are secure in the event of an accident.

Money-Saving Fuel Efficiency

The Sleekster promises financial security as well. Driving this innovative hybrid vehicle, which delivers 39 mpg on the highway, you'll feel good knowing that the money you're saving on fuel can go toward the things that really matter to you.

A Rate Established Exclusively for You

As a preferred customer of Township Motors, you qualify for a private introductory lease rate of $329 per month for 36 months on the Sleekster RS (certain restrictions apply). This offer is valid through March 25, the official date of the vehicle's release.

Please visit www.townshipmotorsco.com and click on "Special Offers" for more details. I will follow up with you in the next week to discuss your plans for your next vehicle and to see where world-class safety and economy fit into the equation.

Regards,

MyName

P.S.: Please keep in mind that this special offer expires just 30 days from now. Contact me at 123-456-7890 or myname@townshipmotorsco.com to schedule a test drive today.

Dear Karen:

This note is to thank you and YourCo for your loyalty to SuperVent, Inc., over the years; we truly appreciate the trust you've placed in SuperVent's HVAC systems for your commercial projects. I'm also writing to let you know that YourCo now has the opportunity to realize even greater operating quality, cost efficiency, and personalized service . . . with an upgrade to SuperVent's new EcoFlowz green HVAC system.

EcoFlowz exceeds the rigorous performance demands of the most modern buildings. With its compact components, the system has a smaller physical footprint, affording your engineers and architects more room to accommodate other critical systems. EcoFlowz is also designed for streamlined operation: Tests confirm that operating noise and emissions are 27% and 34% lower, respectively, than conventional models.

Even more importantly the system's efficient operation translates to lower installation and maintenance costs. On average, efficiency ratings have increased by 43% in buildings where the system has been installed—often representing the margin necessary for commercial projects to ensure profitability.

And as always, these products are backed with the extraordinary levels of customer service, financing flexibility, and technical proficiency that you've come to expect from SuperVent. I can help to work out a plan that fits your budget, our engineers can retrofit the new systems with minimal hassles or disruptions, and our support team can help to optimize the system's operation for years to come.

With this in mind, I will follow up with you in the next couple of days to discuss your evolving needs for heating and cooling—and how SuperVent EcoFlowz systems might fit into your buildings' greener, more efficient future.

Thanks for reading, Karen . . . speak to you soon.

Regards,

MyName

P.S.: Need one more reason to consider upgrading to EcoFlowz? The systems can substantially enhance your buildings' drive toward valuable LEED certification. Let's discuss how this could positively affect your future business endeavors.

The Follow-up: Examples

Subject: An answer for you from PowCo

Dear George:

Thanks for meeting with me yesterday. I know how tough it can be to focus when you get those calls from home (trust me, I know--I have three kids), so I really appreciate your time.

You told me that the two main considerations for metal roofing systems in your commercial projects are weather-proofing and the ability to get curved panels. Today I spoke to Tim Smith of the PowCo product team about the RoofUs 5000 System, and he said, "The system comes standard with XYZ-70 high-performance coating, and we can curve the panels to virtually any configuration."

Based on that information and after watching the video demo that I shared with you, how do feel our systems stack up against your current supplier? What else can I provide that might help with your decision making?

For our next discussion, allow me to treat you to breakfast before work if that's easier for you.

Regards,

MyName

Subject: Following up on Wed. call (SureCo)

Dear Taylor:

This is Steve from SureCo Insurance; I'm following up on our phone call from Wednesday. Thank you for being very honest with me and letting me know that you're in the early stages of researching coverage and shopping around for different providers.

You're probably finding that you have a lot of choices. Given your concern about premium costs, please be sure to ask these different providers about their term life policies. Term insurance might be a good option for you because it allows you to access significant benefits for low premium costs. SureCo, for example, has a low-premium 20-year term policy for a non-smoker in your age range. (Please take a look at the attached comparison of SureCo's term policies vs. other carriers.)

After you've had a chance to review the attachment, when would be a good time for me to check back with you?

Looking forward to speaking with you again.

Best,

Steve

Subject: Next steps after Mon. meeting

Dear Ken:

It's Kim, the business coach. Thanks for meeting with me. Considering all that you have going on, I truly appreciate your time. With that in mind, you told me that layoffs at your company have you working more hours than ever, and it's affecting your personal life. You're hoping to work smarter, reduce your stress level, and achieve more of a work/life balance. These are things I understand intuitively: Having been in that position myself, I researched and developed a sound strategy to achieve an ideal balance.

However, you're wary of business coaching because you feel that most practitioners offer one-size-fits-all approaches. I know this concern, too. A regional manager like you had similar questions before she came to me last year. After a year of working with me, she had this to say: "Kim came up with a plan developed exclusively for me. She took the time to learn my priorities and helped to make connections that I hadn't seen."

If you could meet with me again so that I could put together a complimentary personalized agenda for you, how would that affect your thinking about working with a business coach? I will follow up by phone to discuss, and I promise not to keep you for more than three or four minutes.

Best,

Kim

Subject: Dave from WhizNet on integration, etc.

Dear Thomas:

Thanks for giving me the opportunity to present WhizNet's software solutions for your wireless communications systems. It's always good to talk with another veteran from the early days of SuperZip Technologies. Seems like we both wound up better for the experience!

Just to recap, you said that while the quality of WhizNet's advanced software was impressive, you are more concerned with ease of integration and customization and the responsiveness of tech support. You've got the right priorities here, which is why I'm happy to report that WhizNet's wireless physical layer solutions are built for flexibility: They can be integrated seamlessly into a variety of platforms. And each one is backed by our WN360 Customer Program, winner of the XYZ award for outstanding service.

I have attached some product specs based on the application type you outlined. When you've had a chance to review, let's set aside 12 to 15 minutes to discuss in more detail how WhizNet's offerings align with your requirements for integration and service. When would be a good time for me to check in with you?

Regards,

Dave

The Demo: Example

Subject: See LockDown Security Systems in action

Dear Pam:

Thanks for speaking with me about LockDown Security Systems. From our phone call, it's clear that you are a busy person who's on the road quite a bit. So I wanted to mention one more benefit: If you are out of the house and there's a security breach, the system not only will notify our Emergency Center, but it also will dial up to three mobile phone numbers of your choice. This means that the moment we hear about it, you'll hear about it--giving you even greater peace of mind.

Please take a look at this 60-second video, which shows you how simple it is to set up:

www.youtube.com/4rmrt5fst

Once you've had a chance to view it, let's talk again about how this reliable, convenient system fits in with your mobile lifestyle. I'll check in with you next week.

Regards,

MyName

The Bulletin: Example

Subject: Article in Times: Budget cuts

Dear Sonia:

I heard the news this morning about the go-ahead on the governor's hospital budget cuts. I know that you're probably already huddling about this over there, but I wanted to pass along this article from today's Times, which quotes a spokesperson from Rx10 Healthcare Systems talking about the impact on the company:

www.biggcitytimes.com/hospitalbudgets

We both know from experience that one area inevitably will be hard hit: the hospital's ability to purchase new capital equipment such as X-ray and ultrasound machines. Since you and I are in the middle of planning our partnership for the coming fiscal year, how will this news affect your decision making? We've always found solid alternative solutions in the past when faced with these situations; I hope we can do so again.

I understand that you have much larger concerns to deal with right now, but I consider you a valued business partner and would like to be able to continue serving your needs, no matter what.

Regards,

MyName

The Solution: Example

Subject: Proposal from Lookatme Graphics

Dear Jim:

Thanks for giving Lookatme Graphics the opportunity to bid on a contract for your promotional and trade-show signage needs. I have attached a .pdf outlining our proposal in detail, including full pricing, specs, and warranty information.

Based on our conversations to this point, I understand that your main priorities regarding event signage are

* Maximum quantity/exposure within budget
* Ease of use and portability from event to event
* One-stop resource from design to production

In our proposal, we have put together what we feel is a comprehensive package of solutions that addresses your needs. Here is a top-line summary:

* 20 XYZ vinyl/metal banner stands (31 × 84 inches) @ $112 each: $2,240
* 15 EFG vinyl/metal floor stands (22 × 28 inches) @ $200 each: $3,000
* 5 SWQ metal literature racks (35 × 15 × 9 inches) @ $125 each: $625
* Graphic design, printing, and production services: $2,750
* Delivery of all materials by May 5
* Two-year warranty on all signage

Once you've had a chance to review, please contact me regarding the next steps. I will follow up in the next day or so to confirm that you've seen this message.

Again, on behalf of the team at Lookatme Graphics, I appreciate your consideration, and I look forward to helping YourBrand make a splash in its promotional efforts.

Regards,

MyName

The Ask: Examples

Subject: YourCo and TestMatic: Next steps

Dear Dan:

Thanks for sharing your feedback on YourCo's need for high-quality, cost-effective testing equipment. Now that you've had an opportunity to share TestMatic's formal proposal with the executive team, I'm checking in to find out where we stand in terms of our potential partnership.

To briefly recap, TestMatic is prepared to deliver

* Eight (8) Integrated PXI Chassis at $1,299 each
* Eight (8) SPDT 10A General Purpose Switches at $1,499 each
* Eight (8) Adjustable-Speed Digital Multimeters at $399 each
* One-year consultation contract with our in-house design engineering and test engineering teams ($3,000 per month)
* All testing products shipped by September 30

How are we looking in terms of an agreement? Please let me know if you have any questions at all. I will follow up by phone in the next 24 hours.

Again, thanks for your consideration, Dan. All of us at TestMatic are looking forward to helping you achieve timely, efficient test solutions.

Regards,

MyName

Subject: Following up on Yumm-Co proposal

Dear Gail:

Thank you again for giving Yumm-Co the opportunity to bid on YourCo's food-service operations. You had asked me to check back with you today, now that you have reviewed the proposal with your executive committee. I hope that Yumm-Co's recent on-site presentation captured for you the quality, variety, and efficiency that have made us the fastest-growing full-line food-service provider in the region.

To summarize, Yumm-Co will handle food-service and vending operations at YourCo for a three-year term at a flat monthly rate of $45,000, which includes professional staff and management, all food costs, and labor costs, including taxes, supplies, insurance, and permits. This price is guaranteed for one year.

Based on the full proposal, where do we stand in terms of moving forward with this partnership? In order to build staffing and inventory for the start of your fiscal year, we would need to have an agreement in place fewer than 30 days from now, on September 1.

I will call you in the next 24 hours to discuss. In the meantime, please feel free to contact me with any questions or comments. All of us at Yumm-Co look forward to helping YourCo enhance the quality of life for your employees through healthy, great-tasting culinary choices.

Regards,

MyName

The Negotiation: Examples

Subject: MyChemCo pricing

Dear Andrew:

Thanks for your feedback on the proposal. You mentioned that other suppliers bidding on this contract have not passed along a price increase for the coming year, so you have asked us to waive the stated 2% premium. You've also told me that the specs are equal among the suppliers.

I'd first like to offer some more detail about the new pricing. As you know, our industry has been adversely affected by cost increases in raw materials and energy, as well as surcharges for shipments by rail. The new pricing, effective January 1, reflects this reality. For MyChemCo to maintain the quality of its premium titanium dioxide--including its unmatched gloss and weather resistance--and our track record of on-time shipping, we have made a decision to raise the rate (our first such increase in three years).

While I'm not in a position to speak for the other suppliers, I can promise you that MyChemCo won't sacrifice quality to make up for the added costs of doing business.

That said, I want to make this work for both of us, so let's look at some other ideas. If, for example, MyChemCo were to drop the increase to 1% in exchange for a two-year exclusive contract, how would that affect your pricing concerns?

I'll give you a call shortly to discuss.

Best,

MyName

Subject: Following up on MixoCo price discussion

Dear Louis:

Just a quick note to follow up on our conversation yesterday. I'd like to address your hesitation regarding the prices of MixoCo's Mobile Mixer and Slip Form Paver. You said that the costs are not justifiable within your budget, based on your projected hourly operational use.

First, let me say again that I can certainly understand your concerns, given the unpredictable state of the construction market. I'm confident, though, that we can work through this to generate solid, long-term value for YourCo.

In fact, your idea--that MixoCo extend its all-inclusive warranty beyond the seven-year period--is an excellent start. I discussed this option with my management team today. It is willing to extend the warranty to ten years should you agree to purchase three additional Slip Forms for the Paver at our preferred rate, as outlined in the spec sheet. The value of an additional three years of cost-free maintenance far outweighs the cost of the Slip Forms themselves.

How does this latest proposal line up with your budget expectations? Looking forward to hearing from you.

Best,

MyName

Subject: CompuPhoria proposal - hardware agreement

Dear Marian:

Following up on our phone conversation. Thanks for your candid remarks about CompuPhoria's IT/networking proposal. I respect the fact that you're seeking maximum value for your IT outsourcing budget during what is a challenging time for the industry.

You mentioned that your previous vendor gave you three years of hardware replacement and repair at no additional charge, and you expect the same from us. I've discussed this with my management team, and we are prepared to extend the agreement from two years to three years at no additional fee.

In exchange, we ask that you try our XYZ-Lok security package for three months at the preferred rate of $2,000 per month. It represents a critical component of your IT operations, and its cost is a fraction of the value of the extended hardware agreement.

How does that line up with your thinking? I'll call you tomorrow to discuss in more detail.

Best,

MyName

The Objection: Examples

Subject: PurePower unattended operation

Dear Patricia:

Thanks for your feedback on the proposal from PurePower Gas Generation Systems. I appreciate your concern about the feasibility of running this system unattended because this is a crucial safety and budgetary issue for every organization in our industry.

I can give you these assurances:

* In nearly three decades of service in hydrogen generation, we have never had a single accident.
* Each of our systems is designed to monitor safety parameters continuously; in the unlikely event of a shutdown, an alert is sent out remotely.
* Our experienced field service technicians will help you to integrate the system to your specific requirements, thus minimizing the margin of error.

Given this new information, how would you like to proceed from here?

Best,

MyName

Subject: PosiTruth Drug Assay Kit pricing

Dear Fred:

Thank you for your quick response to the proposal from BigBio Labs. I can certainly understand your concerns about pricing, given our industry's across-the-board rise in screening expenses.

You mentioned the price of PosiTruth Drug Assay Kits in comparison with that of our largest competitor. While I'm not in a position to comment on that firm's pricing, I can tell you that BigBio's patented EZ-Test process delivers more consistent and reliable results vs. our competitor based on the latest clinical studies. Less retesting means greater long-term cost efficiency.

BigBio also can help to mitigate costs on a volume basis. By enrolling in our Customer Loyalty Program (which would kick in automatically by increasing your order to 10,000 kits), you can lower your per-unit rate by a significant 10%.

How does this information figure into your overall view of the proposal? Looking forward to your response.

Best,

MyName

Subject: Following up on Supermega proposal

Dear Betty:

Thanks for your thorough feedback on the Supermega Communications proposal. Your keen eye for detail is something you have in common with those of us on the Supermega team.

You mentioned that you are considering Supermega for brand marketing, but you have no need for public relations because you've been handling that in-house. I would like to point out that the most successful brands consider marketing and public relations to be inseparable, and they rely on experts for both.

You have a major product launch scheduled for the fourth quarter. To achieve early acceptance in the marketplace, it's best to let experienced pros--with extensive contacts in business and consumer media--spread the word.

You've also said that budget is a related concern. So, instead of a monthly retainer for public relations, we can certainly look at a flat-fee model for specific projects, including press releases and media events.

How does this affect your thinking about the proposal? I will call you tomorrow to discuss this further.

Regards,

MyName

The Nudge: Example

Subject: Status on Zippcraft proposal

Dear Henry:

When we last spoke, you mentioned that your upcoming travel schedule was such that you wanted to finalize your plans for fractional jet ownership by the end of the month. Since we're now just a couple of days from that date, I'm checking in to see where we stand in your decision making.

As a quick reminder, Zippcraft is prepared to offer you a share in its program (50 annual occupied flight hours) at a total monthly purchase and operating fee of $20,000, based on a three-year commitment. I have structured this deal to deliver the best possible combination of value and flexibility, as per our conversation.

Given this, would you say that we have an agreement in principle?

Thanks for your consideration. I will follow up by phone tomorrow to discuss how Zippcraft's proposal fits with your timing and business needs.

Best,

MyName

The Close: Example

Subject: Final offer on 123 Main St.

Dear Bart:

I just got off the phone with the selling agent regarding the office warehouse space at 123 Main. They are willing to offer the following:

* They will add two parking spaces, bringing the total to 12.
* They will fix the damaged bay at the rear of the building.
* They are holding firm at $1,250,000.

This is their final offer. We have until noon tomorrow to agree to the deal, or it's off the table, because the other potential buyer is lined up and waiting.

To recap developments on our side:

* You agree that the space is ideal for your business.
* We've gotten them down from $1.5 million.
* Comparable properties in the region are selling for up to 20% higher than that.

Given this, I strongly recommend that you take the offer. What do you say about getting this done?

I will call you shortly to discuss the next steps.

Best,

MyName

The Walk-away: Example

Subject: Recap of Feb. 17th meeting

Dear Derek:

While all of us at Brightenloud A/V Services are disappointed that your committee has turned down our latest proposal, we truly appreciate the opportunity to bid on a contract with Bigstate University. Here is a summary of our final offer:

* 15 flat-screen video monitors
* 15 drop-down screens
* 15 ceiling-mounted overhead projectors
* 15 DVD/VHS combo players
* 15 audio CD players
* 40 wireless handheld microphones
* Includes 2-year equipment lease, staff training, technical support, repair/maintenance
* Total: $450,000

We believe that this offer fully addresses each of the university's needs at a fair price; to lower it further would undercut the value of our services. So at this time we feel that it's appropriate to end discussions.

You did mention that the committee conducts an annual review of its vendors, and there may be an opening for Brightenloud to make a new bid. In the meantime, we are always adding efficient new technologies that reduce operating costs, which could make a difference down the road.

Derek, thank you for your honesty and fairness throughout this process. I will contact you in a few months to discuss developments on both sides.

Sincerely,

MyName

The Commitment: Example

Subject: Agreement: Mallorama Stores and Chic-8 Designs

Dear Melissa:

The entire team here at Chic-8 is thrilled to be entering into business with Mallorama Stores. We look forward to providing you with trend-setting apparel products that fit your customers' lifestyle.

To recap, we have agreed in principle that Chic-8 will deliver the following:

* 1,000 Supra-1 dresses @ $60 each
* 1,000 Mega-7 skirts @ $35 each
* 2,000 Meta-3 tops @ $20 each
* Order delivery date of March 1

A contract is on its way for your approval. If you have any questions, please don't hesitate to call me.

Again, thank you so much for giving us the opportunity to join your prestigious brand roster-- our mission is to exceed your highest standards for quality and service.

Best,

MyName

The Thank-You Letter: Example

Dear Howard:

Just a personal note to thank you again for your business! As a small gesture of my appreciation for your fairness and consideration throughout this process, please enjoy this catered lunch for your staff compliments of MyCorp.

I'm looking forward to working with you and your team . . . and helping YourCo get the most out of this exciting new partnership.

Can't wait to get started!

Best,

MyName

Index

Ralph Allora is the principal owner of Allora Communications, a consultancy specializing in marketing strategy and creative services. Throughout his career, he has delivered on-target promotions and creative messaging for sales professionals under demanding deadlines and high-pressure quotas. His corporate experience includes management and marketing roles at well-known magazine brands such as *Esquire, Motor Trend, Forbes* and *U.S. News & World Report*. His clients have included *The New York Times, The Wall Street Journal, Gourmet*, and *Harper's Bazaar*, while his copywriting work has appeared in publications including *Architectural Digest, Advertising Age*, and *Good Housekeeping*.